Warning!
Revelation Is
About To Be
Fulfilled

Scriptural references, unless indicated, are taken from the HOLY BIBLE: NEW INTERNATIONAL VERSION, Copyright 1973, 1978, 1984 by International Bible Society and published by Zondervan Corporation.

Larry W. Wilson

Wake Up America Seminars, Inc.
P.O. Box 273, Bellbrook, Ohio 45305
(937) 848-3322

First edition, March 1988
Second edition, June 1990
Third edition, January 1991
Fourth edition, November 1992
Fifth edition, June 1994
Sixth edition, June 1997
Seventh edition, June 2002
Eighth printing, June 2004
Ninth printing, June 2005
Tenth printing, August 2007
Eleventh printing, May 2012

Acknowledgments

This book is dedicated to those who are longing for the imminent return of our Savior, our Lord and our Friend, Jesus Christ.

This book has been made possible through the sacrificial generosity of donors who share my hope and joy in the gospel of Jesus Christ. Even though hundreds of thousands of readers will never know the identity of their benefactors, Jesus knows what has been done for His glory and He will reward accordingly.

Special appreciation is due Marty, Shelley, and Suzy for their help on this edition. I am also indebted to a group of enthusiastic volunteers and a growing number of wonderful people worldwide who understand this unique message and faithfully support this ministry.

Wake Up America Seminars, Inc. (WUAS) is a non-profit organization. WUAS is not affiliated with any church nor endorsed by any religious body. Our mission is to proclaim salvation and herald the imminent return of our Lord, Jesus Christ, through whatever means possible.

Warning!
Revelation Is About To Be Fulfilled

Table of Contents

Chapter 1
An Overwhelming Surprise

To the Reader

If separated from the larger context of this book, this chapter could make God appear to be very cruel and unfairly harsh – so please read subsequent chapters as soon as possible! The devil delights in distorting the character of God whenever possible. The devil wants people to see God as a vengeful tyrant or a divine Santa Claus that can do no harm. Of course, both extremes are false. The same God who destroyed the world in Noah's day and sent fiery brimstone upon Sodom and Gomorrah, also sent His Son to die on the cross for our sins. (John 3:16) In short, God reveals His love for the human race in a well-documented balance between justice and mercy. Bible history proves that God is longsuffering. He extends mercy to sinners day after day, year after year – until the day comes when extended mercy no longer has any redeeming effect. Then, God justifiably responds in wrath to deal with defiant rebellion. I offer this introductory statement because the contents of this chapter may seem overwhelming the first time you read it, but please press on and read Chapter 2 as soon as possible.

No Longer a Book of Mystery

The book of Revelation contains several prophecies that integrate into one big story. Some prophecies in Revelation have been underway for centuries and others are about to begin. When we properly assemble all of the prophecies, a mind-boggling drama unfolds. God's ways are wonderful to understand and so thrilling to discover. Some prophecies in Revelation are easy to understand and others are difficult at first, but we can say the same of God. Certain aspects about God are

easier to understand than others. Ultimately, the book of
Revelation confirms the good news that most people want to
hear: A world of eternal joy and endless bliss *is* coming. The
bad news is that God is going to test the inhabitants of Earth
before He sets up His kingdom. (Revelation 3:10) God will
separate "the sheep from the goats" *before* the Second Coming.
The separation of the sheep from the goats is an important
process in God's plan because God will not permit rebellious
people (represented by the goats) to enter His coming kingdom.
God's kingdom is reserved for people who love Him and exalt
His righteous ways. **"Blessed are the pure in heart, for
they will see God. . . . Nothing impure will ever enter it**
[the holy city], **nor will anyone who does what is shameful
or deceitful, but only those whose names are written in
the Lamb's book of life. . . . He will wipe every tear from
their eyes. There will be no more death or mourning or
crying or pain, for the old order of things has passed
away."** (Matthew 5:8; Revelation 21:27, 4, insertion mine)

The book of Revelation reveals that God will soon inflict the
world with a series of 14 plagues. These events will not occur
in random order nor will they be freak disasters caused by
nature. The seven *first* plagues are called "seven trumpets" in
Revelation because they serve the purpose of warning or
awakening the people of Earth to the glorious arrival of Jesus
Christ. The seven *last* plagues are called seven bowls because
they represent seven full cups of God's vengeance that He will
pour out upon His enemies. Although the Bible completely
explains these events, they will come as an overwhelming
surprise for most people. Our Creator has carefully designed
these coming events to achieve His goals, and He will carefully
execute these judgments so that He can redeem the maximum
number of people. As you read this little book, periodically
remind yourself of two things: First, God so loved this world
that He gave His only Son to die in our place and second, God's
patience with defiance and rebellion is limited. During the
Great Tribulation, the people of Earth will see God's perfect
balance between justice and mercy. Remember this balance as

you consider this study about the Great Tribulation. The next few pages give a brief overview of coming events.

How the Tribulation Begins

The Great Tribulation will begin suddenly. It will begin with a global earthquake that effectively disrupts the activities of the whole world. (Revelation 8:5) God has a few things to say to the human race, and He intends to arrest the attention of the world with a massive earthquake that literally stops everything and everyone in their tracks. The sudden cessation of life as we know it will force everyone to stop and wonder what is going on. This coming earthquake is particularly interesting because geologists theorized a "global earthquake" was physically impossible until the early 1990's. Now, physical evidence is proving that Earth's tectonic plates go much deeper into the core of Earth than previously thought, and this information has caused geoscientists to change their thinking. The book of Revelation predicts there will be a total of four global earthquakes. (Revelation 8:5; 11:13; 11:19; 16:18) These earthquakes will increasingly rip up the surface of the world, and the infrastructures of travel, communication and manufacturing will collapse during the Great Tribulation. These earthquakes have no equal in recorded history. Each earthquake will have greater strength than the one before it. The final earthquake will be so violent that it will literally move all of the mountains and islands from their places. (Revelation 16:20; 6:14)

Trumpet #1. Shortly (perhaps 30 days) after the first global earthquake, showers of white-hot hailstones will rain down from the sky. Meteoric firestorms will ignite unquenchable fires all over the world and the accompanying windstorms will destroy billions of acres of trees, food crops and vegetation within a few days. Of course millions of people will be left homeless and many more will suffer and die during this "rain of terror." (Revelation 8:7)

Trumpet #2. A few days after the meteoric showers of burning hail, Earth will experience two horrific asteroid impacts.

The first asteroid will impact an ocean; the second will impact a continent. (Revelation 8:8-11) The first impact will create a series of tidal waves that will inundate coastal cities around the perimeter of the ocean. Seaports and coastal cities, well known for their immoral behavior, will completely disappear with overwhelming loss of life. Survivors will be frightened and distressed by the angry tossing of the sea. (Luke 21:25) Ships will not be able to cross the ocean and men will be powerless to do anything about the churning of the deep.

Trumpet #3. The second asteroid will impact one of Earth's continents with devastating results. The impact will contaminate water supplies and cause extensive death. Ground waves from the impact will fracture geologic strata for thousands of square miles. Sewage, deadly bacteria, toxic chemicals and other garbage buried in the Earth will seep into underground aquifers. Underground rivers will become contaminated and they will carry their deadly mixture for thousands of miles. Revelation predicts that many people will die of drinking poisonous water.

Trumpet #4. Shortly after the second asteroid impact, the world will hear a terrible roar. Hundreds of powerful violent volcanic eruptions will occur. These will be numerous and powerful and cause great damage. Millions of people will perish. Revelation predicts there will be great darkness. (Revelation 8:12) The jet stream will carry megatons of volcanic ejecta and soot around the world in dense clouds that cause complete darkness. Scientists have observed this phenomenon in recent times. The extended absence of sunlight over the middle third of Earth (the breadbasket of the world) will prevent surviving crops from reaching maturity. Worldwide famine will begin.

In short, the first four judgments will create a horrible domino effect radiating into every aspect of life. Illness of all kinds will appear. Clean water and food will become scarce overnight and the misery index will be "off the scale." According to

Revelation, 25% of Earth's population will perish from these four judgments. (Revelation 6:8) Think about this. The population of Earth currently is more than six billion people. Twenty-five percent of six billion people is one billion five-hundred million people!

Trumpet #5. By the time the fifth trumpet sounds, Earth will have experienced a worldwide situation that is so desperate that we can only compare it to the flood in Noah's day. God deliberately puts the whole world in a desperate situation because He knows it is the best way to get everyone's undivided attention. From a parental perspective, God puts the warring nations of Earth in a type of "time out." God wants everyone to consider several issues. For example, God wants the world to know that the time has come for the nations of Earth to end. (See Daniel 2.) He wants everyone to know that He is about to establish His kingdom and He wants everyone to know the terms and conditions of being a part of His coming kingdom.

A few days before the Great Tribulation begins, God will anoint 144,000 servant messengers with exceptional Holy Spirit power. These people, from every nation, kindred, tongue and people, will speak for God for 1,260 days. The 144,000 will be ordinary people who will come from every religious background, and they will harmoniously proclaim the gospel of Jesus Christ to the human race. As strange as it may sound, most of the world's population will reject the terms and conditions of salvation.

About two and a half years after the Great Tribulation begins, God permits that ancient serpent, the devil himself, to appear on Earth physically. The devil will come with millions of angels and he will masquerade as Almighty God. (Revelation 9:1-11; 2 Thessalonians 2:1-12; Revelation 13:11-18) The devil is the dreaded Antichrist. Deceptively cloaked in brilliant light and charming benevolence, the devil will claim that he is God. The devil will declare that he has come to establish a thousand years of peace on Earth. At this time, there will be three identifiable groups of people. The first group of people are those who have rejected the devil and decided to follow the leading of the Holy Spirit. The other group of people will readily receive the devil as God because of the miracles he performs. The third group of people will defy both the devil's demands and the prompting of the Holy Spirit because they refuse to obey anyone. Since God is separating the people of Earth into two camps, sheep and goats, He will allow the devil to inflict great pain and suffering upon this third group of people who have chosen to defy both God's and the devil's authority. Fortunately, the devil will not harm the saints with this affliction. Many of the devil's victims will eventually relent and join the devil's camp. However, a few of his victims will come to their senses, repent of their defiance against the gospel of Jesus and receive salvation. The devil will even call fire down from Heaven to prove his assumed divinity. Consequently, millions of people will ultimately conclude that the devil is God and they will obey him with astounding zeal and devotion.

Trumpet #6. When the devil's popularity and control of Earth reach a sufficient level, he will tell his followers that everyone who refuses to recognize him as God must be annihilated. I call the events of Trumpet #6, World War III. During this time, God will allow the devil and his angels to kill one-third of the world's population. (Revelation 9:15) The devil will establish a one world government and he will exalt himself as King of kings and Lord of lords. He will control all of the necessities of life and if a person wants to buy or sell items for survival, that person must become a member of the devil's kingdom. To demonstrate citizenship in his one world government, the devil will force the inhabitants of Earth to receive a tattoo on their right hand. This tattoo will be the number "666." People who serve as officials in the kingdom of the devil will receive a tattoo on their foreheads to show their superior rank. The tattoo on the foreheads of the devil's lieutenants will be the chosen name that the devil uses. (Revelation 13:17) The placement of a tattoo on the forehead of Satan's lieutenants is a blatant counterfeit of what God intends to do for His faithful servants, the 144,000, after He takes them to Heaven. (See Revelation 14:1; 22:4.)

Trumpet #7. Before Satan implements the mark of the beast, everyone on Earth will have heard the gospel and everyone will have made an informed decision for it or against it. When every person has made a decision, Jesus will close Heaven's door of mercy. Jesus will announce that the offer of salvation is closed by saying, **"Let him who does wrong continue to do wrong; let him who is vile continue to be vile; let him who does right continue to do right; and let him who is holy continue to be holy."** (Revelation 22:11) Then, the second global earthquake occurs. (Revelation 11:19)

Seven "First" Plagues – Seven Trumpets						
1	2	3	4	5	6	7
Global Earthquake #1	Meteoric Firestorm	Asteroid Impact in a Sea	Asteroid Impact on Land	Great Darkness	The Devil Appears	Mark of the Beast Set Up
1260 Days – The Gospel Proclaimed in All the World						

Note: columns 6 and 7 also show "Door to Salvation Closed" and "Global Earthquake #2"

Figure 1.1

World's Infrastructures Destroyed

According to the time periods given in the books of Daniel and Revelation, the first four catastrophic events could occur during a very short period, perhaps 30 to 60 days. The magnitude, extent and rapidity of these horrible events will catch everyone by surprise and they will cause every survivor to ask three questions. First, **"What does God want?"** In ages past, God has sent warning judgments mixed with mercy in an attempt to awaken people to their true condition. (Ezekiel 6; Zephaniah 2) In this sense, the seven trumpets will be no different. By gaining the attention of the world through His wrath, God will put His servants, the 144,000, in an authoritative position to present the terms and conditions of salvation. The overwhelming evidence of God's wrath will be obvious to religious, as well as nonreligious minds. Through a sequence of carefully designed events, God will ultimately separate the survivors of Earth into two categories – those who are willing to submit to His authority and those who defiantly stand in rebellion.

The second question that will come to the forefront of people's minds will be, **"Why is God so angry?"** Great terror will fill the hearts of those who survive the first judgments of God. Every infrastructure will be broken or demolished. Communication, travel, commerce, education, agriculture, healthcare and governmental assistance will be almost nonexistent. The availability of food and water will be questionable. Because the Holy Spirit will empower the 144,000 to proclaim God's Word powerfully, the world will clearly hear *why* God is angry. Everyone, everywhere must hear why God's anger has boiled over. In this painful setting, a third question will rise: **"What is coming next?"** The first four events will cause many to think that God has decided to destroy Earth "a piece at a time." The rich and the poor, the arrogant and the humble, the educated and the uneducated, the powerful and the powerless will be dumbfounded. Depression, anxiety and grief will render many survivors dysfunctional. Few people are mentally or spiritually prepared to cope with the coming tribulation, and physical preparation to save ourselves from God's wrath is useless. Jesus said, **"As it was in the days of Noah, so it will be at the coming of the Son of Man. For in the days before the flood, people were eating and drinking, marrying and giving in marriage, up to the day Noah en-**

tered the ark; and they knew nothing about what would happen until the flood came and took them all away. That is how it will be at the coming of the Son of Man." (Matthew 24:37-39)

If the Bible teaches anything about God's wrath, it reveals that God *always* takes action when a majority of people violate His laws and do evil. The Bible speaks of the flood in Noah's day, the destruction of Sodom and Gomorrah, the destruction of Jericho, the destruction of Jerusalem, and at the end of the age, the destruction of Earth. Revelation predicts that Earth will receive a series of 14 deadly blows. By the time the Great Tribulation has ended, God will have destroyed every defiant person on Earth. These three questions and man's attempt to answer them – within the context of God's cataclysmic manifestations – will produce the human response that Revelation predicts.

Man Responds to God's Judgments

Because God's judgments will be overwhelmingly destructive, world leaders will immediately declare the obvious: "These horrific events are acts of God." Religious leaders from all faiths will sincerely and promptly react by forming a coalition of religions from all nations. This coalition will agree with one voice that God is angry with the whole world. They will also agree that humanity needs a solution to appease God, but the solution will be problematic. Diverse religions do not agree on what is God's will. The Catholic or Protestant view of God is different from the Islamic view. The Islamic view of God is different from the Jewish view, etc. The problem will be simple in definition. Humankind faces *one* angry God, but there are many religions on Earth – each trying to appease God according to its flawed view of God! Revelation calls the initial coalition of religious leaders "Babylon" because it will be totally confused by a membership of diverse religions. (Revelation 13:2-4; 14:8) The word Babylon itself is derived from the word Babel, which means confusion. (Genesis 11:6-9)

Overnight, a religious revolution that springs from fear and terror will catch the world by surprise. God's judgments will harm every nation, state, city and community in some way. The fragile line of separation between church and state, especially in the United States and other western nations, will quickly vanish. The message from the coalition of religious leaders will be simple to understand: "God is angry with our decadence and violence. He has expressed His anger toward man's wicked behavior. We must repent of our sinful ways and worship God or He will destroy the rest of us." The irony in this situation is that the coalition will correctly identify the problem, but their solution will be diametrically opposed to God's will! This is exactly what God wants. God intends to set up a situation throughout Earth where His laws stand in direct opposition to the new laws that the coalition will advocate. This conflict over laws will set a global stage that will show where our highest loyalties lie.

Community Effect

Communal suffering is a powerful force that can bring diverse and antagonistic groups of people together in mutual respect. Sociologists have long noticed this phenomenon. For example, Hurricane Andrew nearly wiped out Homestead, Florida, (USA) in August 1992, but the hurricane actually brought about a new "Homestead," a new community of friendship and caring. Before the hurricane, people lived next door to each other for years without even knowing their neighbor's name. Suddenly, the aftermath of the hurricane placed the survivors "in the same boat together." Talk about "fellow-ship!" The most expensive hurricane ever to hit the shores of the United States may have destroyed the neighborhood, but it formed a community. Neighbors soon discovered that they needed each other to survive – a typical response to shared suffering.

Shared suffering can produce a "communal effect" on a national scale as well. When terrorists destroyed the twin towers of the World Trade Center on September 11, 2001, the United States became a nation of *united* states overnight. For a few weeks, partisan bickering on Capitol Hill ceased. The communal effect produced national unity and because people's minds focused on patriotism, political infighting stopped. Democrats and Republicans even met together on the steps of the Capitol Building for a prayer vigil. They worked together to enact laws *quickly* that would help the FBI and other agencies to root out terrorists that might be lurking in the United States. Citizens proudly displayed the American flag on thousands of buildings and millions of automobiles because a strong wave of patriotic sentiment swept over the nation. These reactions to the terror on September 11 were visible evidences of the "communal effect."

Expressing the scope of these matters in written form is very hard. Worldwide devastation will change everything *overnight*. The fear of God will humble all of the nations of the world for a season. The infighting and bickering of nations will stop. Everyone will realize that there is an Almighty God and the nations of Earth will be forced into realizing that humankind is accountable to Almighty God. (Genesis 6:5,6) In a setting of overwhelming destruction, it is easy to comprehend how global suffering and severe trauma can crescendo into a religious response that will culminate in a community of diverse, but united people.

"Sin Less" Laws

Revelation also predicts the coalition of religious leaders (Babylon) will have very close ties with the political leaders of the world. (Revelation 13:6-8) The religious leaders of each nation will urge its respective law makers into sponsoring laws that will appease God. The result will be the enactment and enforcement of laws demanding that people sin less. Obvious sins such as sexual immorality and other forms of immoral behaviors will be outlawed because religious leaders will argue that humanity cannot appease God unless those who defy God are punished. Christian leaders will use Leviticus 17, Daniel 9, Colossians 3 and other texts in the Bible to prove that God hates sexual immorality, murder, etc., as well as those who stand in rebellion against His laws. They will design these well-intentioned laws to prohibit any action that angers God. Of course, this is where the heart of the crisis forms and it is precisely the conflict that God wants. The laws of man will mandate that God be worshiped in a way that is contrary to His law. The question of survival and a conflict over the worship of God will be the core issues of the Great Tribulation. People will be torn between obeying God's laws (presented by the 144,000) and obeying the laws promoted by the religious leaders of Babylon. (Revelation 13:8) Using this conflict, God will test every person on Earth to see who loves Him more than survival itself.

When fear rules, common sense is usually left behind. In this setting, religious leaders and lawmakers will exert enormous influence and authority over survivors. Due to the chaos caused by the first four catastrophic events, the leaders will establish martial law in all nations. Constitutional rights and privileges, due legal process and other inalienable rights that many nations currently respect will be suspended. Religious leaders will forcefully argue that God is justified in His great anger. (What else could they say – that God is not justified?) With one voice, leaders from all religions of the world will claim that man must repent of his evil ways and worship God. The religious coalition will maintain that God's wrath will cease if there is less sin. Therefore, "sin-less" laws will be necessary. (Since most religious leaders do not understand Revelation's story, they have no idea that God has ordained these 14 judgments.) The world's religious leaders and most of the world's politicians will unite and agree stating, "we cannot tolerate sinful behavior or all of us will perish." Lawmakers will respect the spiritual guidance of their nation's religious leaders and enact laws mandating severe punishment for any person who offends God. (Many such laws already exist in most Islamic countries now.) Religious leaders will use the same argument the high priest used against Jesus, "... It is better

. . . that one man die . . . than the whole nation perish."
(John 11:50)

Opposition

When a crisis arrives, the world will need crisis decision making. Some people will have the courage to speak out and refuse the demands of their government, while others will capitulate under the pressure. As time passes, people will begin to argue over the methods used to appease God and some will dispute the need to mandate righteous behavior through the imposition of law (legislating that God be honored and worshiped). History proves that most people resent having another man's view of God forced upon them. Yet, the smoldering evidences of extensive destruction will be everywhere and government leaders will be looking for expedient ways to restore order. Over time, political leaders will increasingly capitulate to the demands of religious leaders. Like them or not, law enforcement officials will have no option but to enforce the laws enacted by the crisis government. The overwhelming destruction in every nation will silence most of the opposition. After all, what does a world do with an angry omnipotent God?

This may sound surprising, but God's servants will voice the greatest opposition to the "sin-less" laws established by the governments of the world. The 144,000 will speak out against the views and doctrines of the religious coalition (Babylon). The mission of the 144,000 will be threefold: First, they will correctly explain *why* God is doing what He is doing. Second, they will explain *how* people are to worship God, which will be contrary to the laws that religious leaders and politicians have implemented. Third, they will encourage everyone to stand on God's side and *rebel* against the man-made laws that are contrary to the laws of God. The 144,000 will proclaim that everyone who follows the laws of the religious coalition will be worshiping the devil himself, instead of God. (Revelation 13:4) Obviously, people will be listening, observing and considering their powerful confrontation. The Great Tribulation will be a very interesting time.

God's Wrath

At this point in our study, we have summarized very briefly the events surrounding Revelation's story. Now, a few comments are necessary about God's wrath. God has three types of wrath – redemptive, destructive, and annihilative. According to the Bible, God will use redemptive and destructive wrath on Earth *before* Jesus appears at the Second Coming. The seven first judgments (seven trumpets) are redemptive in nature. The idea is simple: God mixes mercy with His judgments so that, if possible, many people will choose salvation and be redeemed. God will use redemptive judgments to open the minds and ears of billions of people to consider a gospel that is different from anything they have ever heard. He will use 144,000 people anointed with Holy Spirit power to preach the everlasting gospel and millions of people will receive Jesus Christ as their Savior. Unfortunately, an even larger number of people will reject the gospel and rebel against the authority of the coming King. After 1,260 days, God will terminate His offer of salvation and God will implement a second type of wrath. This wrath is called "destructive wrath." (Genesis 6:5-7; Revelation 15:1; 16:1-21) When sinful behavior goes beyond the point of redemption, God cauterizes the growth of sin with total destruction and He starts over. The flood demonstrated this type of wrath in Noah's day, and it also explains the total destruction of sinful nations and empires since. God will use this type of wrath during the seven last plagues or the seven bowls. (Revelation 15:1) The third type of God's wrath is "eternal annihilation." God has never implemented this type of wrath on Earth before. At the end of the one thousand-year millennium, God will resurrect all of the wicked. They must stand before the judgment bar of Christ and hear why He has refused to grant them eternal life. After the wicked confess that Jesus was righteous and fair in His decision, God will punish the wicked and totally annihilate both sin and sinners. **"And whosoever was not found written in the book of life was cast into the lake of fire. . . . Blessed are they that do his commandments, that they may have right to** the tree of life, and may enter in through the gates into the city. For without are dogs, and sorcerers, and whoremongers, and murderers, and idolaters, and whosoever loveth and maketh a lie." (Revelation 20:15; 22:14,15, KJV, insertion mine) The topic of God's wrath is enormous and it requires study to understand the right balance between God's mercy and God's justice. This topic is covered in more detail in my book, *Jesus, The Alpha and The Omega.*

The Whole World Tested

The book of Revelation describes the seven trumpets and the seven bowls as seven *first* plagues and seven *last* plagues. These 14 events will not happen in random order nor will they be random manifestations of nature. Jesus told His disciples, **"I have told you now before it happens, so that when it does happen you will believe."** (John 14:29) Because the Bible gives the order of coming events in 14 steps, it is possible to identify and anticipate each phase of the Great Tribulation. If knowing the order of events is important, knowing the purpose of each step is even more important. Each person needs to know that God has deliberately and purposefully designed the Great Tribulation to accomplish several strategic objectives. The Bible indicates that God initiates the Great Tribulation, God controls the 14 steps of the Great Tribulation, and God terminates the Great Tribulation. God is Sovereign and He has several marvelous objectives that He will achieve during the Great Tribulation. For example, God has predetermined that the Great Tribulation will be a time of confrontation. A sovereign and righteous God plans to confront a world of many religions, cultures and languages with three simple truths. The 144,000 will present Bible truth which will confront thousands of errors. People who love God and seek to know His truth will submit to God's truth and receive eternal life. Many people who know nothing about God will turn to Him during Earth's last hours and be saved! Others who hate God's authority and His truth will defy the authority of God and rebel against God's laws. Even though there are more than six billion people living in more than 220 nations on Earth, God has a very clever plan that will test everyone in every religion in the same way! (Revelation 3:10) According to Revelation, this is the process:

The first four trumpet judgments will overwhelm and startle everyone on Earth. The amount of destruction and loss of life will put the whole world in a state of shock. The fear of God will be a literal reality. The survivors of the first four judgments will intellectually and emotionally react. God will use His redemptive wrath and man's reaction to His judgments to set up a very important test throughout the world. God wants His laws to stand in direct opposition to the laws of man. This juxtaposition will put every person in a difficult situation because rebelling against God will have severe consequences and rebelling against the laws of man will also have severe consequences. By setting up a global situation where there are only two options – obey the laws of God and suffer the wrath of man, or obey the laws of man and suffer the wrath of God – the innermost allegiance of every human being will be revealed.

God will set a situation in motion in every nation that will reveal who is willing to obey Him, even if it puts people at odds with their family, their religion and the laws of their government. By doing this, God will determine who loves Him and His truth above everything else. God has designed the Great Tribulation to be a great controversy and the Bible reveals how this controversy will end. There will be enormous casualties on both sides of the controversy, but God will triumph in the end because He is omnipotent. He has the power of resurrection! (Revelation 19:20,21; 1:18)

Chapter 2
The Full Cup Principle

God's Love Poorly Understood

The Bible declares that God is love, but God's love is poorly understood today. (1 John 4:7,8) The meaning of *love* is so distorted by sin that many people do not understand what love is! When God sends His judgments upon the nations of Earth, one of the most difficult things the 144,000 will have to explain is that God is love! How will people reconcile "God is love" when the smoldering evidences of His wrath are lying all around?

God's love is revealed in a perfect balance between justice and mercy. Because of sin, man's sense of balance between justice and mercy has become distorted and inadequate. We cannot see everything that God sees and our limited view makes trusting an infinite God very hard sometimes. God understands our limitations, but He requires His children to trust Him implicitly. He alone knows the best way through the corridors of life to eternity. His laws reflect His infinite knowledge. Few people spend time trying to understand God's laws, mercy, justice, authority, glory and power, but this will change when God releases His wrath. Stunned by chaos and destruction, people will open their Bibles and discover a diary of God's actions covering thousands of years. God's policies are changeless because God does not change. It is ironic, but during the time of God's wrath, many people will learn what divine love is all about and, for the first time, experience a saving relationship with God. (Jeremiah 29:13)

God allowed the prophet Isaiah to see certain aspects of His glory, yet Isaiah was amazed at God's reluctance to show Himself to the world. He wrote, **"Truly you are a God who**

hides himself, O God and Savior of Israel." (Isaiah 45:15)
God's *apparent* silence in the affairs of humankind is a consequence of sin. Most people know that inappropriate behavior
can separate friends and family members from each other. The
same is also true of God. Sin is so offensive to God that it has
separated us from His presence. As generations come and go,
the reality of God becomes dimmer. As knowledge about God
becomes faint, and the longer we go without renewed evidence
of God's authority and glory, the more silent He appears to be.
In the vacuum of this silence, sin becomes more attractive and
less offensive. Wicked people become bold and defiant in their
transgressions. Violence, sorrow and suffering spring up like
dandelions after a spring rain. Every night, the evening news
confirms the human race is wallowing in the slime of depravity. Degenerate, even hideous sins are either glamorized,
justified or treated as inconsequential on television. Sin is like
the drug novocaine – it deadens our sense of fairness. Sin
causes us to minimize the suffering that results from our deeds
and to avoid, at all costs, any penalty for wrongful behavior.
(How many people in prison falsely maintain their innocence?
How many people in prison would be willing to stay in prison
and pay the full price for their deeds if they had the option to
get out?) Because of sin's deadening power, people can commit a horrible deed and then convince themselves they did not
do it or justify their behavior for doing it. Such is the power of
sin. From the very beginning, sinners have been reluctant to
accept their responsibility for sin. Lucifer blamed God. Our
parents, Adam and Eve, also deflected their responsibility for
sin in the Garden of Eden. (Genesis 3:12,13) Even though sin
has great control over sinners, the power of sin can be broken.
Whenever a sinner is "born again" by Holy Spirit power, the
first thing a saint wants to do is to take responsibility (and
provide the necessary restitution) for his or her sin.

God Will Not Be Silent Forever

The Bible confirms that God breaks His silence from time to
time by using one or more of His four deadly judgments to
limit the growth of sin. (Ezekiel 14:21) The four judgments He

uses are sword, famine, plague and wild beasts. (Revelation 6:8) In His infinite wisdom, God allows a nation to have power until it fills up its cup of iniquity, and when it does, the Bible says He removes that nation from power. (See Daniel 2:21; 4:17; Leviticus 18:24-28.) What makes this process so remarkable is that God, even within the chaos of sin, always accomplishes His plans and purposes on Earth! We may try to explain the outcome of earthly events by analyzing the actions of the players, but this remains a limited view. Do not be naive and think that things just happen because of the prowess of human beings. Nothing happens in the universe without God's knowledge and permission. Even though we are not able to see God on His throne, we can know that He reigns over the kingdoms of man. God is Sovereign. We may not see all that He is doing, but the evidence is right before our eyes. The Bible is crystal clear. God is in control. (Job 38) How He maintains control is a mystery. That He does it without showing Himself is His silence.

God's silence is not impossible to penetrate if you really want to see and hear Him. The evidences of His handiwork are all around us if we want to acknowledge Him. However, if we choose not to give Him respect, we can easily ignore Him and deny the recognition He is due. Thus, His silence complements our power of choice. God can either be the greatest and most wonderful Being in all the universe, or if we so choose, we can deny His existence. What a God! Perhaps the least understood element within God's character is His reluctance to awe His creatures with His power and presence. His silence will be a topic of eternal discovery!

Very Important Point

God will soon break His silence with the first global earthquake. (Revelation 8:5) When Earth's inhabitants experience God's coming judgments, God's love and His purposes will be grossly misunderstood and misrepresented. The religious leaders of the world will encourage politicians to enact laws "honoring and appeasing the God of Heaven." However, mandating righteousness cannot accomplish what God wants! God is more interested in true repentance and a submissive attitude from His children. He wants men and women to recognize His sovereignty, not for who He is, but for *what* He is and what He represents. God is love. He calls men and women to live a life free from the damning power of sin. Even more, He will grant His power to everyone so they can be victorious over sin. He wants us to overcome our carnal nature and rebellion against His boundless ways of life. Inconceivable as it may seem, Revelation predicts that the majority of men and women will reject God's terms and conditions for salvation during the Great Tribulation. Hardened by lifelong rebellion, the hearts of many people have become so numbed by sin that even God cannot reach them. If a person's heart cannot be reached through love and patience or through redemptive judgments, how can God produce a broken heart and a repentant spirit within a sinner?

Revelation describes how wicked people will be filled with a spirit of hatred when confronted with the truth about God and His will. God will initiate this confrontation when He selects and anoints 144,000 servant-prophets to speak on His behalf. These spirit filled people will proclaim the gospel to the inhabitants of every nation. Evil men will punish and torture God's servants because their message will openly reveal man's rebellion against God. God's messengers will be in direct conflict with those who govern a world that currently belongs to Satan. (Luke 4:5-6) The persecutors of God's servants will think, like Pilate, that they can wash their hands from the guilt of these acts. Yet, God *never* ignores evil, even though He may allow it to flourish for a time. Eventually, God will avenge every evil deed and He will be sure that wicked people receive a double portion of pain in return for the pain they have inflicted. (See Revelation 18:6, 2 Corinthians 5:10 and Obadiah 1:15.)

In the context of His coming judgments, God's character and His behavior will be grossly misrepresented and misinterpreted. This is the heart of Revelation's story. It is a story of a patient God visiting a planet in deep trouble. It is also a story about rebellious people and a world gone astray. Most people, when put to the coming test, will openly and willfully reject the clearest evidences of God's truth and God's sovereignty. They will unite themselves in rebellion against the laws of the Most High God by first obeying the laws of the land and then, the laws of the radiant being, the Antichrist – the devil himself. About two and a half years after the Great Tribulation begins, God will allow Satan to physically appear before the people of Earth because **"they refused to love the truth and so be saved."** (2 Thessalonians 2:10-11) Jesus said, **"This is the verdict: Light has come into the world, but men loved darkness instead of light because their deeds were evil. Everyone who does evil hates the light, and will not come into the light for fear that his deeds will be exposed."** (John 3:19-20)

The Full Cup Principle

The Bible says that God is love. (1 John 4:8) The Bible also says that God has wrath. (Colossians 3:5,6; Revelation 15:1) Because God's character has both properties, it is sometimes difficult to reconcile these two attributes. So, let us consider how the perfect balance works between God's love and God's wrath. Bible history reveals that God follows a consistent principle when dealing with humanity. I call this principle the "full cup principle" because the Bible often uses the metaphor of a cup to indicate the fullness of an experience. For example, consider the words of Jesus just before He was arrested and crucified, **". . . My Father, if it is possible, may this** [bitter] **cup be taken from me. Yet not as I will, but as you will."** (Matthew 26:39, insertion mine) Jesus did not want to endure the experience of a bitter death on the cross, but He was willing to do it if this was the only way to save the human race. The metaphor of a cup can be used to indicate a joyful experience. Consider David's well known words, **"You prepare a table before me in the presence of my enemies. You anoint my head with oil; my cup** [of joy] **overflows."** (Psalm 23:5, insertion mine) King David uses the metaphor of an overflowing cup to express joy beyond containment! From these two examples we see that a cup represents an experience. The contents of the cup indicate the type of experience.

Notice how God used the metaphor of "the cup" in Jeremiah's day: **"This is what the Lord, the God of Israel, said to me: 'Take from my hand this cup filled** [to the brim] **with the wine of my wrath and make all the nations to whom I send you drink it. When they drink it, they will stagger and go mad because of the sword I will send among them.' So I took the cup from the Lord's hand and made all the nations to whom he sent me drink it:"** (Jeremiah 25:15-17, insertion mine) Now, compare Jeremiah's words with the warning words of God's servants, the 144,000 in Revelation 14: **". . . If anyone worships the beast and his image and receives his mark on the forehead or on the hand, he, too, will drink of the wine of God's fury, which has been poured full strength into the cup of his wrath. He will be tormented with burning sulfur in the presence of the holy angels and of the Lamb."** (Revelation 14:9,10) This text points forward to a time during the Great Tribulation when people will be warned about worshiping the Antichrist. Everyone who submits to the laws of the devil will have to drink from the cup of God's wrath.

The full cup principle is based on the idea that God *measures* the actions of mankind. Every time we do wrong, we add a sin to our cup of grace. When all of God's grace has been displaced by willful sin, our cup becomes full of bitterness and we have to drink the consequences of our actions. When God forces people to reap what they have sown, He is returning to them what they deserve. (Galatians 6:7) The golden rule is an iron clad rule. It says: As we do unto others, the same will be done to us. (Matthew 7:12; Obadiah 1:15) Because God acts on this principle, He is said to have vengeance. (Romans 12:19; Revelation 2:23)

In a similar way, God *measures* the actions of nations. Do you remember the words Daniel spoke to King Belshazzar the night he saw the handwriting on the wall? Daniel said, **"This is what these words** [on the wall] **mean: Mene : God has numbered the days of your reign and brought it to an end. Tekel : You have been weighed on the scales and found wanting. Peres : Your kingdom is divided and given to the Medes and Persians."** (Daniel 5:26-28) Babylon had filled its cup and God responded. God's patience with man's arrogance and defiance has limits. When the cup of transgression is nearly full, God breaks His silence by sending a warning through His selected messengers. If the warning does not work, He then uses one or more of His four deadly judgments (sword, famine, plagues and wild beasts – Ezekiel 14:21; Revelation 6:8). If the situation is redeemable, His judgments are redemptive. If the situation goes beyond re-demption, His judgments are totally destructive. Remember, the coming events predicted in Revelation will be divided into two groups of seven. The first seven plagues (seven trumpets) will be redemptive. The seven last plagues (seven bowls) will be totally destructive.

Many people currently interpret God's silence or passiveness with evil to mean that He is either nonexistent or indifferent to what we do. Others see His permissiveness as proof that He is not interested in each person's day to day activities. For this reason, a growing number of people are committing horrible, evil deeds, thinking that God does not see them and will not hold them responsible for their actions. Many people do not realize the strict accountability that each of us must give to God for every action! Solomon said, **". . .Fear God and keep his commandments, for this is the whole duty of man. For God will bring *every deed* into judgment, including every hidden thing, whether it is good or evil."** (Ecclesiastes 12:13,14, italics mine)

Examples of the Full Cup Principle

The people in Noah's day filled up their cup: **"The Lord saw how great man's wickedness on the Earth had become, and that every inclination of the thoughts of his heart** was only evil all the time. The Lord was grieved that he had made man on the Earth, and his heart was filled with pain. So the Lord said, 'I will wipe mankind, whom I have created, from the face of the Earth men and animals, and creatures that move along the ground, and birds of the air for I am grieved that I have made them.' " (Genesis 6:5-7) God destroyed the world with a flood in Noah's day when the antediluvians' cup of iniquity had reached full measure. God broke His silence through Noah by warning the world about His forthcoming actions. Then, when 120 years had expired, He destroyed all but eight of the inhabitants of the world. When extended mercy fails to produce repentance and reformation, as with the antediluvians, God's justice demands destructive action.

The Amorites filled up their cup: **"Then the Lord said to him (Abraham), 'Know for certain that your descendants will be strangers in a country not their own, and they will be enslaved and mistreated four hundred years. But I will punish the nation they serve as slaves, and afterward they will come out with great possessions. You, however, will go to your fathers in peace and be buried at a good old age. In the fourth generation your descendants will come back here, for the sin of the Amorites has not yet reached its full measure.' "** (Genesis 15:13-16)

Notice the last sentence of the previous text. God promised to give Canaan to Abraham's offspring only after the sins of the Amorites had reached their full measure! Make no mistake about this. Canaan belongs to the Creator, and He promised Canaan to Abraham's descendants only after the Amorites had exhausted their chance for possessing that beautiful land. Keep in mind that Israel's possession of Canaan was based on the same conditions that applied to the Amorites. Contrary to what a lot of people think today, Israel's possession of Canaan has always been conditional. Moses warned Israel: **"But be assured today that the Lord your God is the one who goes across ahead of you like a devouring fire. He will** destroy them; he will subdue them before you. And you will drive them out and annihilate them quickly. . . . After the Lord your God has driven them out before you, do not say to yourself, 'The Lord has brought me here to take possession of this land because of my righteousness.' No, it is on account of the wickedness of these nations that the Lord is going to drive them out before you. It is not because of your righteousness or your integrity that you are going in to take possession of their land; but on account of the wickedness of these nations . . . ." (Deuteronomy 9:3-5) This is an extremely important point: The Canaanites were also driven out and/or destroyed when they filled their cup of wickedness! When God's patience with the Canaanites reached its limit, He broke His silence by sending wrath upon them! (Leviticus 18:24-25)

The nation of Israel filled its cup with sin: Just before the Babylonian captivity (605 B.C.), God told Israel, **"But you did not listen to me . . . and you have provoked me with what your hands have made, and you have brought harm to yourselves. . . . Because you have not listened to my words, I will summon all the peoples of the north and my servant Nebuchadnezzar king of Babylon . . . and I will bring them against this land and its inhabitants and against all the surrounding nations. I will completely destroy them and make them an object of horror and scorn, and an everlasting ruin . . . This whole country will become a desolate wasteland, and these nations will serve the king of Babylon seventy years. But when the seventy years are fulfilled, I will punish the king of Babylon and his nation, the land of the Babylonians, for their guilt . . . and will make it desolate forever."** (Jeremiah 25:7-12)

According to Jeremiah 25, Israel was destroyed for provoking God to anger and the prophecy in Jeremiah 25 also predicts the destruction of Babylon at a time in the future! This proves that God deals fairly with all nations. In God's eyes, wickedness is wickedness. Each person, city, nation and kingdom has a cup and when it becomes full, God breaks His silence. Because God is always consistent, we discover an interesting truth. Civilizations rise and fall by divine decree. When the Babylonian empire's cup became full, God destroyed the empire and gave it to the Medes and Persians. When the time came for Babylon's destruction, based on the full cup principle, it occurred because God made it happen. The time will come when God will destroy the whole world so Jesus can come and establish an eternal kingdom of righteousness and peace! This too, will occur because God will make it happen!

New Testament Examples

The full cup principle concept is also confirmed in the New Testament. Paul warned the sexually immoral Romans, "**. . . you are storing up wrath against yourself for the day of God's wrath, when his righteous judgment will be revealed. God will give to each person according to what he has done. But for those who are self-seeking and who reject the truth and follow evil, there will be wrath and anger.**" (Romans 2:5,6,8) Compare these verses with Paul's statement in 2 Corinthians 5:10: "**For we must all appear before the judgment seat of Christ, that each one may receive what is due him for the things done while in the body, whether good or bad.**" Paul understood why God's wrath is coming. He told the believers in Colosse, "**Put to death, therefore, whatever belongs to your earthly nature: sexual immorality, impurity, lust, evil desires and greed, which is idolatry. Because of these, the wrath of God is coming.**" (Colossians 3:5,6)

Paul encouraged the believers in Thessalonica to be patient in their suffering until the enemies of Christ had filled up their cup. "**. . . You suffered from your own countrymen the same things those churches** [in Judea] **suffered from the Jews, who killed the Lord Jesus and the prophets and also drove us out. They** [the Jews] **displease God and are hostile to all men in their effort to keep us from speaking to the Gentiles so that they may be saved. In this**

way they always heap up their sins to the limit. The
wrath of God has come upon them at last." (1 Thessalonians 2:14-16, insertions mine) When Paul wrote this epistle, he
knew the Jewish nation had filled up its cup of sin and he
knew that God was sending the Romans to destroy Jerusalem.
Rome destroyed Jerusalem in A.D. 70 just as Jesus had pro-
phesied. (Matthew 24:1,2; Luke 21:22)

Jesus and the Full Cup

Jesus explained the full cup principle in a discourse with the
Pharisees. After pronouncing seven curses on the Jewish
leaders for their religious bigotry and hypocrisy, Jesus said,
**"Fill up, then, the measure of the [cup of] sin of your
forefathers! You snakes! You brood of vipers! How will
you escape being condemned to hell?"** (Matthew 23:32,33,
insertion mine) Again, the point is made: When a nation or
individual reaches the limit of divine forbearance, God breaks
His silence. His mercy with sin and sinners has a limit. Jesus
concluded His denunciation of the Jewish nation by saying, **"O
Jerusalem, Jerusalem, you who kill the prophets and
stone those sent to you, how often I have longed to
gather your children together, as a hen gathers her
chicks under her wings, but you were not willing. Look,
your house [temple] is left to you desolate."** (Matthew
23:37,38, insertion mine) Later, Jesus predicted Jerusalem's
destruction as a fulfillment of God's wrath: **"When you see
Jerusalem being surrounded by armies, you will know
that its desolation is near. Then let those who are in
Judea flee to the mountains, let those in the city get out,
and let those in the country not enter the city. For this
is the time of punishment [wrath] in fulfillment of all
that has been written [in the Scriptures concerning Israel]."**
(Luke 21:20-22, insertions mine)

Does God Kill People?

From time to time, scholars and pastors assert that God does
not kill or destroy people. They defend this by saying that, (1)
God does not violate His own commandment, **"Thou shalt not**

kill" (Exodus 20:13, KJV), and/or (2) God just steps aside and turns evil people over to the natural consequences of sin which brings death and destruction. In simple terms, advocates of this view reason that if God is love, He does not violate His character of love by doing evil (e.g., killing). (1 John 4:8) Instead, God simply steps out of the way when people become totally evil. He either allows sin to take its natural, destructive course or He turns them over to the devil – allowing Satan to do whatever he wishes. The justification used to support either position is false.

A person cannot understand aspects of God's character and ignore His own words! Notice what the Lord *Himself said* in the days of Noah, **"The Lord was grieved that he had made man on the earth, and his heart was filled with pain. So the Lord said, 'I will wipe mankind, whom I have created, from the face of the earth – men and animals, and creatures that move along the ground, and birds of the air – for I am grieved that I have made them.'"** (Genesis 6:6,7) The Bible puts God in an active role – not a passive position concerning the destruction of Earth at the time of the flood. Notice the same position of God with respect to the destruction of Sodom and Gomorrah: **"Now the men of Sodom were wicked and were sinning greatly against the Lord. . . . Then the Lord rained down burning sulfur on Sodom and Gomorrah – from the Lord out of the heavens. Thus he overthrew those cities and the entire plain, including all those living in the cities – and also the vegetation in the land."** (Genesis 13:13; 19:24,25) Centuries later, Jude warned early Christians saying, **"In a similar way, Sodom and Gomorrah and the surrounding towns gave themselves up to sexual immorality and perversion. They serve as an example of those who** [will] **suffer the punishment of eternal fire** [that will come down from God out of Heaven]." (Jude 7, Revelation 20:9 insertions mine) One more example is included to show how God Himself is willing to destroy nations when necessary. The Lord *said* to

Israel at the time of the giving of the covenant at Mount Sinai: **"If in spite of these things** [redemptive judgments] **you do not accept my correction but continue to be hostile toward me, I myself will be hostile toward you and will afflict you for your sins seven times over. And I will bring the sword upon you to avenge the breaking of the covenant. When you withdraw into your cities, I will send a plague among you, and you will be given into enemy hands."** (Leviticus 26:23-25, insertion mine) There are many more examples in the Bible, but these should be sufficient to show that God not only kills people for justifiable reasons, but He takes full responsibility for doing so.

Falsehoods about God's character do a lot of damage when they contain some truth. (A good lie is 99% truth.) The Bible says that God is love. Jesus' death on Calvary *proves* that God is love. What more could He do than live among the stench and rejection of sinners for 30 years and then give His life for us? Not only did He make eternal salvation possible, but He gives us grace to meet the challenges of each day. He provides food and clothing for us, He sustains us because He cares for us and desires the best for us. He even knows the number of hairs on our heads. (Matthew 10:30) The problem though, is that God's love does not lessen the importance of His boundaries between good and evil. (Genesis 2:17) God requires man to live within boundaries He has established – both physical laws and moral laws. For example, consider the physical law of momentum: Mass times velocity equals momentum. A 4,000 pound car going 60 miles per hour has a lot of momentum. Suppose a man drinks too much, gets drunk and while driving his car at a high rate of speed hits a tree and dies. Did God kill the driver? No. The law of momentum produced the injury that caused death. So, there is validity to the claim that sin has consequences. But the question remains, did a loving God create the law of momentum that killed the drunk driver? Yes, God created the law of momentum and He wants us to live within the boundaries of that law. If a man chooses to get drunk and drive his car into a tree, then it is fair to conclude that the drunk killed himself. The other motorists can consider themselves very fortunate if the drunk kills only himself or herself!

Regarding this issue, many people stumble over the sixth commandment, **"Thou shalt not kill?"** Does God violate His own commandment when He kills people? This is a good question. Let us examine the *intent* of the commandment, **"Thou shalt not kill."** God has declared that there are a few circumstances where death can be inflicted upon a person (as in capital punishment) without breaking the *intent* of His law. Notice what the Lord told Noah at the time of his exit from the ark: **"And for your lifeblood I will surely demand an accounting. I will demand an accounting from every animal. And from each man, too, I will demand an accounting for the life of his fellow man. Whoever sheds the blood of man, by man shall his blood be shed; for in the image of God has God made man."** (Genesis 9:5,6) This verse indicates that God not only commanded, but expected other men to put murderers to death. *Capital punishment is not man's invention.* The Bible reveals that capital punishment originated with God – not man. (See also Leviticus 20.)

In the wilderness, God not only spoke the Ten Commandments to the children of Israel, He also elaborated on the terms and conditions for capital punishment. **"These are to be legal requirements for you throughout the generations to come, wherever you live. Anyone who kills a person is to be put to death as a murderer only on the testimony of witnesses. But no one is to be put to death on the testimony of only one witness. Do not accept a ransom for the life of a murderer, who deserves to die. He must surely be put to death."** (Numbers 35:29-31) The point is that God does not break the *intent* of His own law by requiring men to put murderers to death. A person has to incorporate *all* that God has said about killing to understand the *intent* underlying the laws that govern life and death. When God said, **"Thou shalt not kill,"** He was forbidding premeditated murder. However, if someone chose to commit murder, God declared that the murderer must be put to death and the next of kin could kill the murderer without incurring guilt. Notice, **"[If] the avenger of blood finds him** [the murderer] **outside the city** [of refuge], **the avenger of blood may kill the accused without being guilty of murder."** (Numbers 35:27, insertion mine) If sinful people can kill a wicked person without incurring guilt under lawful circumstances, God can too.

Underlying Principles

The underlying principles behind capital punishment are atonement and restitution. God requires atonement and restitution for every sin. In God's order, there is no forgiveness for sin. Now, before you jump to any hasty conclusions, keep on reading. I am not saying that sinners are not forgiven. I am saying that sin itself is not forgiven. At first, this statement seems contradictory, but this is what atonement is all about. Atonement for sin is possible only after restitution has been made. It is for this very purpose that Jesus died on the cross. God placed our sins upon Jesus and He was slain in our place. Jesus was our atonement! We may "say" that our sins are forgiven, but this is not the whole story. The sins of all believers are transferred to Jesus, the Lamb of God, when we put our faith in Him as our means to salvation. He is our atonement for sin through faith. If the Old Testament sanctuary service teaches us anything, it is this: God requires atonement for all wrong doing. **"For the life of a creature is in the blood, and I have given it to you to make atonement for yourselves on the altar; it is the blood that makes atonement for one's life."** (Leviticus 17:11) **"In fact, the law requires that nearly everything be cleansed with blood, and without the shedding of blood there is no forgiveness."** (Hebrews 9:22)

A Few Examples

Individuals who claim that God does not kill people cannot give a Scriptural reason for the death of the firstborn, both men and animals, at the time of the Exodus. The Lord warned Moses that if the destroying angel did not find blood on the doorposts, He Himself would slay the firstborn of each family, whether man or animal! **"On that same night I will pass through Egypt and strike down every firstborn both men and animals and I will bring judgment on all the gods of Egypt. I am the Lord."** (Exodus 12:12, italics mine) This is an important point. Who claims responsibility for killing the eldest (the highest ranking) family member of men and animals in Egypt? Who spoke to Moses? If we make the devil responsible, then we must conclude that (a) the devil is speaking in Exodus 12, or (b) God and the devil were partners in the killing of the firstborn.

God does not need or use the devil to accomplish works of righteousness. Furthermore, if God simply turned His back on the firstborn in Egypt and allowed the devil to kill this select group of people, then God should be considered an accomplice to murder. (God says that if an individual has the opportunity to prevent harm and does nothing about it, he becomes an accomplice to the harm committed and shares in its guilt. Ezekiel 3:17-21) The real point is, "Do we take God at His word?" Notice what the Lord told Moses: **"See now that I myself am He! There is no God besides me. I put to death and I bring to life, I have wounded and I will heal, and no one can deliver out of my hand."** (Deuteronomy 32:39)

The deaths of the firstborn in Egypt reveal something important about the character of God. He gave Pharaoh and his court nine plagues (nine chances) to convince them that He was Sovereign, but Pharaoh refused to recognize God's authority. So, God sent a tenth plague upon Egypt which killed many, including Pharaoh's firstborn. During the Great Tribulation, history will be repeated. God will provide an abundance of evidence that He is sovereign, but millions of people will refuse to obey the commands of the Almighty and they will receive His seven last plagues! When men and women refuse the clearest evidences of God's will, what more can He do? What are God's options if individuals willfully refuse to recognize the difference between right and wrong? God killed Egypt's first-born as an object lesson for Israel and to punish Egypt. Egypt's punishment was due to open rebellion against the authority of God. Pharaoh had filled his cup! The object lesson for Israel was even more impressive! The "passing over" pointed forward to a time when God would pass over every human being in judgment to verify that the blood of His sacrifice on Calvary was on the door posts of the heart. (2 Corinthians 5:10) The death of the firstborn in Egypt was a shadow of the death of God's only Son that would be necessary for man's salvation. (The story of Abraham's willingness to offer Isaac as a sacrifice on Mount Moriah reveals the same concept. God tested Abraham's faith to see if Abraham was willing to do to his own son what God would have to do to His Son.) No wonder Jesus is called the Lamb of God. (John 1:29) Incidently, the New Testament describes three instances in which people were killed outright under interesting circumstances. Read Acts 5:1-11 and Acts 12:23 and see if you can determine who did the killing. Also, carefully examine 2 Kings 1:1-17 and determine who destroyed 102 men with fire. Then, read Isaiah 37 and pay close attention to verse 36 where you will discover who killed 185,000 men. These texts should help to dismiss any doubt you may have on this compelling subject.

God's Wrath Will Be Revealed in Our Day

"I the Lord have spoken. The time has come for me to act. I will not hold back; I will not have pity, nor will I relent. You will be judged according to your conduct and your actions, declares the Sovereign Lord." (Ezekiel 24:14) When the Lord spoke these words to Ezekiel, He was referring to the fact that Israel had filled its cup. Our day is coming, too. God will break His silence and demonstrate His animosity toward sin. It will happen suddenly, severing the past from the oncoming future. Life as we know it will immediately and irrevocably change. The world has never witnessed anything like the coming judgments of God, nor can it sustain more than one visitation. God will act suddenly and powerfully, and all the inhabitants of Earth will be overwhelmed with His swiftness and intensity. In this context, the authority, character and actions of God will become the subject of profound interest and controversy among all the people of Earth.

Chapter 3
The First Four Trumpets

Now that we have had a brief overview and justification for what God is about to do, we need to back up and examine the first four trumpets of Revelation in greater detail. During the Great Tribulation, believers will be able to see the fulfillment of prophecy right before their eyes. People who are led by the Holy Spirit will be able to see a distinct correlation between current events and God's Word. Unfortunately, many of the survivors will refuse to understand God's actions because they have hearts like Pharaoh. (Remember the hardness of Pharaoh's heart? Even after God sent ten plagues upon Egypt, Pharaoh refused to submit to God's authority.)

The cause and purposes of the Great Tribulation can be understood by anyone who sincerely wants to know God's ways. If the books of Daniel and Revelation remained obscure and mysterious forever, the final generation would not have confidence in the Bible. Nothing is more powerful than a truth whose time has come. This fact will soon stand in direct opposition to the claims of the world's greatest skeptics. Indeed, you can be sure of this development: Many scientists will deny that the first four trumpet events are "Acts of God." Instead, they will say that these calamities are nature's random curse which *they* have been foretelling for years. On the other hand, leaders of the worldwide religious coalition (Babylon) will claim that these events are judgments sent by an angry God. What a debate! Who will win in the court of public opinion – science or religion? Revelation reveals that religion will once again overpower science and politics! The last time this happened, the age that followed was called "The Dark Ages."

A Great Earthquake

"And I saw the seven angels who stand before God, and
to them were given seven trumpets. Another angel, who
had a golden censer, came and stood at the altar [of
Incense]. He was given much incense to offer, with the
prayers of all the saints, on the golden altar before the
throne. . . . Then the angel took the censer, filled it with
fire from the altar, and hurled it on the Earth; and there
came peals of thunder, rumblings, flashes of lightning
and an earthquake." (Revelation 8:2,3,5, insertion mine)

These verses describe the end of Jesus' intercessory service on
behalf of Earth. In other words, when God's patience with
Earth as a *corporate body* reaches its limit because Earth's cup
of iniquity is full, His wrath toward Earth begins. When the
angel casts the censer down, four physical phenomena will
occur on Earth: thunder, rumblings, flashes of lightning and
an earthquake. Notice also that when God's patience with
individuals on Earth reaches its limit at the end of the seventh
trumpet (at that time every person will have received or rejected the gospel), these same phenomena occur again. Then
again, when the seventh bowl is poured out on the wicked
during the seven last plagues, these four phenomena occur a
third time. These global events, described three times in Revelation (Revelation 8:5,7; 11:19; 16:17-21), are magnificent
signs marking specific milestones in this sequence of 14 events.

The physical signs that mark the beginning of the Great Tribulation will be awesome and they are carefully designed and
implemented to arrest the attention of billions of people. They
will be so powerful that everyone on Earth will shudder. The
global earthquake that marks the beginning of the Great
Tribulation will be distinguished from previous earthquakes on
Earth in two ways:

1. This earthquake will be accompanied by manifestations in
the Heavens and within the Earth. There will be rumblings or
noises that come from deep within the Earth (sounding like
groaning and voices), deafening peals of thunder and a scary

display of lightning – these episodes will be simultaneously heard and observed around the world.

2. This earthquake will cause overwhelming damage throughout the world. Skyscrapers will topple. Vital bridges will vanish. Highways will be broken up. Power grids will be ripped apart. Water lines and septic systems will be broken. The oceans will churn violently. The Richter scale cannot measure the power of a global earthquake and analysts will not be able to calculate the resulting damage. This is too much for man to measure!

Showers of Fiery Meteors Fall

"Then the seven angels who had the seven trumpets prepared to sound them. The first angel sounded his trumpet, and there came hail and fire mixed with blood, and it was hurled down upon the earth. A third of the earth was burned up, a third of the trees were burned up, and all the green grass was burned up." (Revelation 8:6,7)

A few days after the global earthquake and a physical display of God's powers, Revelation predicts much of Earth will be set on fire by a giant firestorm of burning hail (small meteorites). The fiery hail will ignite unquenchable fires all over the world, burning up a third of the trees and all the green grass! The possibility of this happening is not as far fetched as it may sound. Our planet routinely experiences meteoric hailstorms every year. The Leonids, the Perseids, the Lyrids, and the Geminid meteoric showers are annual events that happen when Earth passes through fields of space debris. The gravity of Earth and the orbit of the debris gives the appearance of "shooting stars," but the shooting stars are white hot chunks of space debris. As the debris enters our atmosphere at speeds that may exceed 60,000 miles per hour, atmospheric friction causes the debris to become white hot. So far, these annual displays have not been a serious threat. The white hot debris usually does not reach Earth, but the story will be quite different when the first trumpet judgment occurs.

Think of the consequences when millions of white hot rocks rain down on Earth. We may have a good example of the consequences. Some scientists now believe that the great Chicago fire (October, 1871) was not caused by Mrs. O'Leary's cow kicking over a lantern, but by a shower of fiery meteors. Historical evidence indicates that a string of fires were ignited along a straight line stretching about 200 miles across the north central part of the United States that *same* night. In fact, the entire town of Peshtigo, Wisconsin, mysteriously caught fire and burned to the ground that night. Survivors of the Peshtigo fire reported seeing streaks of fire falling out of the sky. What caused all of these enormous fires to start during the same hour that evening? Scientists believe a shower of white hot hail falling to Earth resolves the question and satisfies the details.

Great Ball of Fire #1

The judgment that follows the firestorm of burning meteors is an asteroid impact. John writes, **"The second angel sounded his trumpet, and something like a huge mountain, all ablaze, was thrown into the sea. A third of the sea turned into blood, a third of the living creatures in the sea died, and a third of the ships were destroyed."** (Revelation 8:8,9)

This scene describes a large asteroid, the size of a mountain, hitting the sea. The term "mountain" is an accurate term for a large asteroid. If an asteroid, one mile in diameter, was sitting on the surface of the Earth, it would be called a *mountain* 5,280 feet high! Even more, John's description of an asteroid impacting the sea is identical to scientific models created at several universities during the past ten years. For example, the tidal wave caused by a great asteroid impact would destroy ships for hundreds of miles in every direction – even those docked in remote seaports. Think about the commotion of the ocean after such an impact! (See Luke 21:25.) According to studies conducted at the University of California, an asteroid of this magnitude would be so hot by the time it hit an ocean that it would make a large part of the ocean water anoxic (oxygen deficient) by simply boiling the oxygen out of a large area of the sea. Sea temperature would rise dramatically and the hot water would kill billions of sea creatures in a very large radius. The warmed, anoxic water resulting from the impact would also provide a perfect environment for the growth of red algae or what is known as red tide. When John said the sea turned to blood, he may have been describing the appearance of red algae, which thrives in oxygen deficient water!

Great Ball of Fire #2

The next judgment is a great asteroid impact on a continent. John describes a great star that impacts the Earth. **"The third angel sounded his trumpet, and a great star, blazing like a torch, fell from the sky on a third of the rivers and on the springs of water – the name of the star is Wormwood. A third of the waters turned bitter, and many people died from the waters that had become bitter."** (Revelation 8:10,11)

Many prophecy experts insist on a symbolic interpretation of these verses, maintaining that they do not believe these events could be literal. However, two compelling reasons eliminate the possibility of a symbolic interpretation. First, each event is physically consistent with the literal outcome John describes. Second, if these texts are symbolic, where is the explanation or interpretation of these symbols within the Bible? How can symbolic people drink symbolic water?

Suppose a large star (asteroid or comet), blazing like a torch, were to impact one of Earth's seven continents. What would be the consequences? Computer and seismic models created at the University of Southern California at Berkeley indicate that ground waves would shear water wells and sewer lines for hundreds of miles in all directions. Earthquakes and tremors would continue for many days as enormous tectonic forces beneath the surface of the Earth adjust to the impact. Of course, everything within two hundred miles of ground zero would be vaporized. Remember, a large asteroid impact would release the energy of thousands of nuclear bombs. This energy would be dissipated in powerful earthquakes and one of the first casualties of such an impact would be drinking water. Broken septic systems and toxic waste buried in landfills would leach into underground rivers that flow into huge aquifers that provide drinking water for millions of people. The results will be devastating. Revelation 8:10,11 predicts that many people will die from drinking bitter water that has become unsafe; a direct consequence of a "star" hitting Earth! The title of this star is very meaningful. **"And the Lord saith, Because they have forsaken my law which I set before them, and have not obeyed my voice, neither walked therein; But have walked after the imagination of their own heart, and after Baalim, which their fathers taught them: Therefore thus saith the Lord of hosts, the God of Israel; Behold, I will feed them, even this people, with wormwood, and give them water of gall** [poison] **to drink."** (Jeremiah 9:13-15, KJV) If we compare the Lord's comments to Jeremiah with John's vision, it becomes clear why the asteroid is called "Wormwood." "Wormwood" means poisonous.

Scientists Predict

In the early 1980's, few geologists and geoscientists accepted the theory that giant asteroids, the size of mountains, had previously impacted our planet. Today, with the help of computers, satellites, and better equipment, scientists have discovered several enormous impact sites on planet Earth. Funny, isn't it, how scientific discovery can reverse long standing conclusions in a very short amount of time! The notion that Earth has been pummeled by giant asteroids was regarded as scientific lunacy in 1978 when geoscientist Dr. Luis Alvarez (University of California at Berkeley), advanced the idea that dinosaurs may have become extinct due to a giant asteroid impact millions of years ago. Dr. Alvarez and other scientists, such as the late Dr. Eugene Shoemaker (1928-1997) from the United States Geological Survey, were among the first geoscientists to conclude that Earth had been impacted by large asteroids. The idea, widely controversial in the late 70's, is widely accepted today due to overwhelming evidence. When the comet, Shoemaker-Levy 9, broke up and impacted Jupiter's surface in July 1994, all arguments ended. One impact site on Jupiter was wide enough to comfortably accommodate two planets the size of Earth side by side. Today, geoscientists are convinced that our planet has experienced horrific impacts from large asteroids and they are just as convinced that our planet will be impacted again. Because erosion constantly changes the face of the Earth, it was difficult to detect impact craters until the late 1970's. Even more, 75% of Earth's surface is covered with water, making it almost impossible to detect ocean impact sites. With the help of satellite photographs, it has become much easier to find these ancient impact sites.

In fact, scientists have identified more than 150 land-craters caused by asteroid or meteorite impacts. The three largest craters are found in Canada, South Africa and off the eastern coast of Mexico. Each of these craters has a diameter of about 120 - 150 miles. The largest known crater within the United States is about 18 miles wide and is located close to Manson, Iowa. Even though craters are sprinkled over various continents, few are as distinct in appearance as Meteor Crater in Arizona. According to Richard A. F. Grieve, Ph.D., a scientist with the Geological Survey of Canada (*Scientific American,* April 1990), the "tiny" iron meteorite which caused Meteor Crater in Arizona was less than 200 feet in diameter and weighed approximately one million tons. It hit the Earth traveling about 35,000 miles per hour (mph) and released energy equivalent to the most powerful nuclear devices available today. Meteor Crater is about two-thirds of a mile wide and 640 feet deep.

The amount of damage caused by an impact is relative to the momentum and the direction of impact. Earth is traveling about 72,000 mph in its annual orbit around the Sun. If a meteor traveling at 40,000 mph hits "head on" with Earth, the energy released would be equivalent to a 112,000 mph collision! *National Geographic* featured an impressive article titled

"Extinctions" in its June 1989 edition, which reported the findings of scientists studying the effects of ancient asteroid impacts. This article is still timely since the Bible and scientists agree that Earth will be impacted again.

The *National Geographic* article proposed the following scenario: "Giant meteorite strikes Earth, setting the planet afire. Volcanoes erupt, tsunamis crash into the continents. The sky grows dark for months, perhaps years. Unable to cope with the catastrophic changes in climate, countless species are wiped off the face of the planet." (page 686) The article goes on to suggest that great fires resulting from an asteroid would destroy crops, trees and vegetation. Even worse, wind storms created by the fires would destroy buildings hundreds of miles from the impact. Dust and smoke from the fires would find their way into the jet stream and block much of the Sun's light, thus altering the world's climate and the chances of human survival!

Will Asteroids Impact Earth Again?

"Sooner or later, it is inevitable," scientists say, "that Earth's gravitational field will attract one or several of these celestial bodies." "Civilization threatening" asteroids (rocks having a diameter of one to 10 miles) are so tiny in space that scientists rarely detect their presence until they are very close to Earth. Scientists calculate that Asteroid 1989 FC missed Earth by only six hours on March 23, 1989. They also maintain that it is highly probable that it will return at some point in the future and this time be even closer to Earth! What is shocking about Asteroid 1989 FC is that it was not detected until after it had passed by Earth. On January 7, 2002, a small asteroid (2001 YB5) about 1,000 feet in diameter missed Earth by twice the distance between the moon and Earth. Although this may sound like a safe distance, the asteroid was traveling *toward us* at 70,000 miles per hour. In other words, we missed an impact by only a handful of hours! This asteroid will revisit our place in space in about 3 years and 7 months since the writing of this book. A document on the NASA internet site currently states that Earth's closest miss with an asteroid has been only a matter of minutes! One asteroid whizzed within 62,000 miles of Earth!

"It is inevitable," scientists say, "Earth will once again be hit by an asteroid large enough to cause mass extinctions . . . ." (*National Geographic,* January 1985, page 47) Scientists Clark Chapman and David Morrison startled 4,000 geoscientists at the American Geophysical Union in San Francisco in December 1989, saying, "In terms of risk, the significant danger [from asteroids] comes from impacts with global implications. Statistically, the greatest risk to each of us is [that] . . . the impact could cause a global disruption of crops and/or food distribution systems, leading to widespread starvation and perhaps the death of most of the Earth's human population. We call this a civilization threatening impact." At the time of the meeting (1989), Dr. Chapman was a scientist at the Planetary Science Institute in Tucson, Arizona, and Dr. Morrison was chief of the Space Science Division at NASA's Ames Research Center in Mountain View, California.

Scientists have known for years that asteroids and meteorites strike the Earth and moon in predictable patterns. In fact, if Asteroid 1989 FC had hit Earth, Dr. Bevan French, an expert at NASA's Solar System Exploration Division, calculated it would have released energy equivalent to 20,000 hydrogen bombs. If it had hit a metropolitan area such as Tokyo, Los Angeles or New York, millions of people would have died instantly. Fortunately, most meteorites that have impacted the Earth in recent times have been small and have had no significant consequence. However, the media reports fireballs and meteorites regularly. As an example, on November 22, 1996, a "small" meteorite impacted Honduras, making a crater 150 feet in diameter.

Sun, Moon and Stars Go Dark

"The fourth angel sounded his trumpet, and a third of the sun was struck, a third of the moon, and a third of the stars, so that a third of them turned dark. A third of

the day was without light, and also a third of the night."
(Revelation 8:12)

The judgments of God do not end with two asteroid impacts.
The fourth judgment follows the first three trumpets and the
result is that the Sun, moon and stars go dark. It is conceiv-
able that the darkness John saw is similar to what occurred in
the northwestern part of the United States during the Mount
St. Helens eruption in 1980. At midday, it looked like midnight. There was no light. Although Revelation does not say
why the Sun, moon and stars turn dark, this worldwide phenomenon would be consistent with volcanic eruptions. The
cumulative effects of a giant earthquake and two asteroid
impacts could certainly disrupt the fragile balance of Earth's
tectonic plates. As the tectonic plates strain to readjust, enormous energy would be released. Hundreds of volcanoes could
erupt, belching magma and ash in a series of explosions that
would dwarf the blasts of Mount St. Helens, Mount Pinatubo
in the Philippines and Mount Popo in Mexico.

Consider the cumulative effect. The first three trumpets send
megatons of dust, soot and debris into the atmosphere. Hundreds of volcanic eruptions (around the Ring of Fire) belch
more dust in the form of volcanic ash, causing extended darkness around the world. Millions of burning acres and resulting
windstorms insure that the jet stream is affected. One ounce of
soot absorbs 25,000 times the amount of sunlight that one
ounce of dust absorbs! Given this physical fact, it is not hard to
see how a band of darkness captured by the jet stream could
encircle the middle third of Earth where two-thirds of the
world's population lives! The absence of sunlight for an extended period of time will produce famine. While you are
pondering these powerful displays of God's wrath, keep in
mind that God is righteous and He can justify His actions.
What does the severity of God's actions say about man's rebellion?

John predicts, **"A third of the earth was burned up, a
third of the trees were burned up, and all the green**

grass was burned up." It is very interesting to note that the quantity of "one-third" is used 12 times throughout the description of the seven trumpets:

> 1/3 of Earth will be burned up
> 1/3 of the trees will be burned up
> 1/3 of the sea will turn into blood
> 1/3 of the sea creatures will die
> 1/3 of the ships on the sea will sink
> 1/3 of the rivers and springs will become contaminated
> 1/3 of the light from the Sun will be taken away
> 1/3 of the light from the moon will be taken away
> 1/3 of the light from the stars will be taken away
> 1/3 of the day will be without light
> 1/3 of the night will be without light
> 1/3 of mankind will be killed in the sixth trumpet war

What is God trying to tell us about the repetitive use of "one-third?" Would you believe it has to do with God's generosity? God destroys one-third, but spares two-thirds. To appreciate the importance of God's generosity, notice how rebellion was addressed in Bible times.

When a tribal nation refused to pay tribute to a king who claimed higher authority over their territory, it was a common practice for the offended king to attack the defiant city and totally destroy it – men, women and children. (Deuteronomy 2:34; 3:6) However, if the king was in a generous mood, he might spare one-third of the nation from destruction (and thus maintain some of his tax base). Notice how this happened during the reign of King David. **"David also defeated the Moabites** [who had refused to pay him tribute]. **He made them lie down on the ground and measured them off with a length of cord. Every two lengths of them were put to death, and the third length was allowed to live. So the** [surviving] **Moabites became subject to David and brought tribute** [tax]." (2 Samuel 8:2, insertions mine)

God also dealt with Israel in a parallel pattern. God tolerated Israel's rebellion for many centuries, but when its cup reached

full measure, God killed two-thirds of Israel when He sent His
servant Nebuchadnezzar to destroy them. (Jeremiah 25:9)
Because God is a generous King, He spared one-third (the
survivors) by putting them in Babylonian exile. God told
Ezekiel, **"A third of your people will die of the plague or
perish by famine inside you; a third will fall by the
sword outside your walls; and a third I will scatter to
the winds and pursue with drawn sword."** (Ezekiel 5:12)
Did you notice God's use of His deadly judgments: sword,
famine and plague? Did you notice that two-thirds were killed?

Again, the balance of mercy can be observed in the days of
Zechariah. God said, **" 'In the whole land,' declares the
Lord, 'two-thirds will be struck down and perish; yet
one-third will be left in it. This third I will bring into
the fire; I will refine them like silver and test them like
gold. They will call on my name and I will answer them;
I will say, "They are my people," and they will say, "The
Lord is our God." ' "** (Zechariah 13:8,9)

The repetitive use of "one-third" within the seven trumpets
declares God's generosity with a defiant and rebellious world.
The trumpet judgments are redemptive in nature. If a generous king spared one-third of a rebellious nation in ancient
times, what can be said of the King of kings who spares two-
thirds of the elements mentioned in the seven trumpets? In
fact, if God justifiably destroyed two-thirds of the items described in the first four trumpets, life on this planet would
perish within a couple months!

Same Conclusions and Some Predictions

What makes this interpretation of the first four trumpets so
uncanny is that scientists and Bible students are not only
arriving at the same conclusions – that asteroids and meteorites will impact Earth – but they are also surprised by the
consistent harmony of results. Will Earth be pummeled by
fiery rocks raining from Heaven? More and more scientists are
convinced it is inevitable, and so are students of Bible prophecy.

Chapter 4
The Human Response

If my conclusions about the first four trumpets are accurate, the book of Revelation will make a lot of sense *just as it reads*. God's judgments initiate the Great Tribulation and they serve as a catalyst to achieve the human responses that God desires. In effect, His judgments and show of force will either harden people's hearts or open their minds. Revelation's story describes how the two phases of God's wrath (redemptive and destructive) will be implemented, and fortunately, it also includes the human response. Revelation predicts the behavior of religious and political leaders who will occupy positions of power when the Great Tribulation begins. The Bible does not tell us who the world leaders will be, but God knows them by name. Two thousand years ago, when John received the visions of Revelation, God foreknew who the political and religious leaders would be. He also foreknew their reactions to His actions and He included their response in the book of Revelation for our benefit. God wants His children to know what they are about to face. Jesus told His disciples, "... **The knowledge of the secrets of the kingdom of heaven has been given to you, but not to them.**" (Matthew 13:11)

So far, we have studied the full cup principle and the first four trumpet judgments. We have learned that when God's patience with the people of Earth reaches its limit, He sends warnings. Bible history indicates God's most effective warnings are those that include both destruction and a message. If there is just a message (as in Noah's day), few believe. If there is destruction but no message, few understand. So, the Great Tribulation includes both.

Global Ruin

God uses the trumpet judgments to warn the world that He is terminating this age of sin. God's spokespersons, the 144,000, will tell a surprised world that He is about to establish His kingdom of righteousness. They will call on everyone to worship God and to reject the claims of Babylon. Of course, all who refuse to obey the laws of Babylon will suffer the consequences. At this point, we have only scratched the surface of all that Revelation has to say. In order to further develop the prophetic story, consider the following scenario. It describes man's desperate situation shortly after the Great Tribulation begins:

The great earthquake that marked the beginning of the Great Tribulation will have ripped up thousands of miles of highways, collapsed overpasses and bridges, and stopped most transportation. The fiery meteor showers that follow will set wildfires that rage out of control for several months. Men will not be able to contain or stop the fires because transportation is completely disrupted. Because one-third of Earth's oxygen producing trees are burned up in the first judgment, respiratory ailments will become a problem for almost everyone. When the damage caused by the raging fires is compounded by two mega-asteroid impacts, any optimist would seriously doubt the possibility of survival on Earth. Scientists have rightly called these large asteroid impacts "civilization threatening impacts." With megatons of ash from the fires and debris from the asteroid impacts circulating in the atmosphere, the added darkness caused by numerous volcano eruptions will make life on Earth a short term situation at best. Furthermore, thousands, perhaps millions of people will die from drinking contaminated water. This means that typhus and other plagues will be rampant. God carefully designed the first four judgments of the Great Tribulation to show the survivors that planet Earth is doomed. Even more, He wants the world to understand the curse of sin. God hopes that when people finally realize that their planet is fatally wounded, they will thoughtfully consider their desperate need of a Savior.

Famine

Even if food crops survive the wildfires, asteroid impacts, and volcano eruptions, few crops will reach maturity after the fourth judgment occurs because sunshine will not be able to penetrate the enormous clouds of ash and soot. Crops will wither and die, especially crops like corn which require 100+ days of sunlight between the last frost and time of maturity. Within a few months, food will be as scarce as gold. (At the beginning of 2002, experts calculate the world's stockpile of food can last about 45 days.) In addition to the famine in the part of the world specifically affected, there will be no rain in many other parts of the world as well! (Revelation 11:6) To make matters worse, scientists claim that rain occurring after a major asteroid impact will become so acidic that it will be lethal to plant and animal life. Obviously, a person does not have to be a rocket scientist to understand that Earth will be damaged beyond recovery. God wants it this way. God is deliberate and purposeful in everything He does and He inflicts a mortal blow to Earth because He wants to send a *strong* message to the survivors.

From man's point of view, desperate circumstances call for desperate efforts. To stabilize their situation, governments will respond. First, they will put emergency constitutions in place. They will declare martial law to prevent anarchy and a complete breakdown of orderly conduct. Stringent laws and curfews will be implemented and people will have no choice but to comply. Many individual freedoms and rights will be suspended. The price of sin is always great – even on the innocent.

To prevent looting and gouging, the nations of the world will implement rationing. People, full of fear, will do anything to obtain food, water and medicine. Governments will control the buying and selling of all commodities. This will be necessary because every survivor needs a basic number of items to sustain life itself. Who can argue with these drastic methods if it means survival? As days turn into weeks and weeks into months, millions of people will give in to depression and despair. Hope for recovery will dim. All parts of the world will have smoldering destruction and suffering beyond description. The nations of Earth will be in a state of shock. People who are alive will envy the dead. Jesus saw the travail of the human race during the Great Tribulation. He said, **"For then there will be great distress, unequaled from the beginning of the world until now – and never to be equaled again. If those days had not been cut short, no one would survive, but for the sake of the elect those days will be shortened."** (Matthew 24:21,22)

Most Important Questions

This is terrible to say, but it is true. When humanity is forced to feel God's wrath, it begins to consider the presence and reality of God. When times are good, God is forgotten. God's love and patience with sinners (God's silence) is misinterpreted. But when God initiates global suffering, suddenly many questions will arise. "Why did God do this? What does He want?" Overnight, a great awakening will occur. At the present time, Christians talk about God's love, the idea of a pretribulation rapture, and God's wonderful salvation and forgiveness, but they do not often talk about the things that make Him angry. Some Christians even deny that God has wrath! Consequently, His judgments will confound many Christians. They will be unable to reconcile these "Acts of God" with their assumed knowledge of God. Their "faith" will disappear when they actually experience God's wrath and terror will overwhelm them.

It is not difficult for God to frighten people. He only needs to tamper with those things that make us feel secure. With many millions of people dead and the scale of destruction beyond measurement, survivors will be forced to acknowledge they do not understand God or have a relationship with the Almighty. Did you notice a knee jerk phenomenon after the terrorist attack on the United States on September 11, 2001? Church attendance popped up 300% for about six weeks! Like Israel of old, nations will tremble with fear before Almighty God during the time of His visitation. (Exodus 20:18-21) The solution to pleasing or appeasing God – so that His destruction of Earth will stop – will appear simple on the surface. Religious leaders will demand, "We must submit to the authority of God." But how does a person worship and honor the God of Heaven so that His righteous wrath will cease?

Religious Revolution

If the physical destruction on Earth and the loss of life caused by the first four trumpets is overwhelming, the religious revolution that follows will seem just as overwhelming. Leaders from all religious systems will unite and with one voice they will offer a straightforward explanation of God's judgments. They will adjust their prophetic interpretations to fit an unfolding situation. They will say, "These 'Acts of God' have come because we have forgotten our Creator." In a sense, this is true! All around the world, religious leaders of all faiths will agree with one another saying, "We must repent of our great sins and appease God or we will be totally destroyed." For authority, Catholic and Protestant leaders will turn to the Bible, Moslems will appeal to the Koran, Jews will appeal to the Talmud, and Hindus and Buddhists will use their holy writings. The point is that every nation will discover its guilt before God and the accuser will be each nation's religion!

As people begin to link the devastations caused by the four trumpets to the idea that God is displeased with the entire human race, one question will form on everyone's mind: "What must we do to appease God before He kills the rest of us?" Even though different solutions will be offered in different nations, a common theme will develop around the world. In fact, Revelation predicts there will be a sudden, but powerful movement to appease God. This movement will have great authority and power. Like religious powers of ages past, it will persecute everyone who refuses to cooperate with it. This movement is called "Babylon" in Revelation because it will be full of confusion. This may read like a fairy tale, but when you think about it, all prophecy seems strange until the time for fulfillment arrives. Currently in the United States, less than 33% of the population attends church regularly. I believe this percentage will more than double when God's wrath is revealed! Religion will become "the" priority and religious leaders with evangelical fervor will lead the nations of the world into a religious revolution.

Number One Question

The coalition of the world's religious leaders will discover a big problem. There are several different religious systems on Earth and each religious group worships God in a different way. *Is there one right way to worship God?* Moslems believe that God is pleased when people obey the teachings of Mohammed and regard Friday as a holy day. Catholics, Anglicans, most Protestants, Greek and Russian Orthodox Christians believe that God is pleased when people obey their religious leaders and the laws of their churches, which includes observing Sunday as a holy day. Jews read the Torah and regard Saturday as a holy day. Hindus, Buddhists and other religious groups have different ideas about what pleases God. Does God really care about the way we worship Him? This question regarding worship will be the subject of much debate. In today's context, the question has no solid footing. At best, it remains one man's opinion against another. However, when 1.5 billion people lie dead among the smoldering ruins that burn the nostrils and eyes of the survivors, how God wants to be worshiped will become *the* question to answer.

"Sin Less" Laws

In an earlier chapter, we discussed the community effect. We know that desperate circumstances can unite a diverse group of people when they share in common suffering. During the Great Tribulation, most people will regard God as a Holy Terror. Religious leaders will easily motivate their frightened government leaders to quickly enact laws that require all citizens to honor and worship God. At first the laws will be oriented as "sin less" laws, but eventually, more laws will be implemented in every nation demanding that everyone respect

God or suffer the penalty. However, there will be no consistency in the legislation of these "sin less" laws; instead, there will be great confusion. Catholics and Protestants will seek laws that agree with their theology, Jews will make laws agreeing with their doctrines, Moslems will want laws respecting their beliefs in Allah, and other groups will do the same. How can diverse religions on one planet appease one God? Is He a God of many religions?

One World – One God – Many Religions

One organization on Earth stands head and shoulders above all others in terms of *diplomatic ties* with religious and political leaders all over the world. It is the papacy. The Roman Catholic Church has steadily secured diplomatic connections with almost every segment of Earth's population since John Paul II became Pope in 1978. When he dies, his legacy to the Church of Rome will be his worldwide pursuit of formal relationships with many countries, which now numbers over 170 nations!

When the seven trumpets begin, the pope in office will move quickly to convene a "World Council" of religious and political leaders. This council will form a powerful coalition that is called "Babylon" in Revelation. (Revelation 13, 17, 18) Perhaps the United Nations will be used to expedite this organization. However, the "glue" that will bond the leaders of the world together will not be politics. Instead, it will be immediate concerns about God's anger and His overwhelming destruction. Overnight, a new reality will settle in on humanity. The old paradigms are out, and new ones will form. In an effort to appease God on a global scale, religious leaders will quickly compromise on "minor" religious differences. The leaders will struggle to find a global solution to appease God, but will be unable to find one. The central question remains: "How does God want the inhabitants of Earth to worship Him?" Moslems, Jews, Catholics, Hindus, Protestants and other religious organizations will have fundamentally different answers to this question and *it will be impossible for one person to prove the superiority of his religion over another.* Thus, a reign of confusion will begin. Eventually, the devil himself will appear on Earth during the fifth trumpet. Masquerading as God, he will solve the solution to Earth's diversity by declaring all of the world's religions void. In their place, the devil will offer his new "one world" religion and the world's religious leaders will zealously participate! After all, they will "think" this glorious being is none other than God Himself!

What Does God Actually Want?

God wants the human race to worship Him – our worship is the only thing in the whole universe that God does not own! God does not need our adulation. Instead, He has given human beings the power of choice and He wants us to choose to worship Him. God wants us to love, adore and worship Him because whatever we worship we imitate! "By beholding we become changed." God wants people in His coming kingdom who uphold and exalt the same laws that He upholds and exalts! So, God will send His servants, the 144,000, throughout the Earth to present His message and purposes. They will present the terms and conditions for salvation. God does not send the first seven judgments upon Earth without a clearly expressed message, for if He did, there would be no meaning or purpose for all the suffering. Remember, the seven trumpets are redemptive in nature. During the 1,260 days of the seven trumpets, God will send three messages throughout the Earth. The 144,000 will present God's first message saying: **"Fear God and give him glory, because the hour of his judgment has come. Worship him who made the heavens, the Earth, the sea and the springs of water."** (Revelation 14:7) Notice the first sentence. "Fear God" will be easy after experiencing some of His power. Notice the second sentence. "Worship Him" will be difficult because worshiping God will be contrary to the laws of Babylon. Also, notice how the last sentence itemizes the four elements that God has afflicted with the first four trumpets! Religious people worldwide will quickly agree why the judgments of God are falling. However, the command to worship God will be the frustrating part. The

144,000 will tell the world *how* God wants to be worshiped, but the leaders of Babylon will also be telling the world *how* to worship God and the two "hows" will be in direct conflict! When all the varying views from the religions on Earth are merged in a context where worship is required, it is easy to see how the world will become a very confusing place during the Great Tribulation.

Think about this for a moment. Sincere people all over the world worship God according to the dictates of their conscience and worship in a way that they believe is true worship. The Bible indicates that God accepts such worship. According to Romans 2, Romans 14, John 4 and Acts 10:35, God accepts the worship of all sincere people on Earth *if* they worship Him in spirit and in truth. If people worship God with a humble and obedient spirit, according to all the truth they know, then God, who is always generous and merciful, accepts their worship as genuine. However, during the Great Tribulation, God is going to send illuminating truth through His 144,000 messengers, telling the world how He wants to be worshiped. People who honestly worship God in Spirit and truth will conform. Everyone else will rebel. As the honest in heart begin to worship God according to His law, their actions will violate Babylon's law. Worshipers will have to disobey the laws of Babylon in order to worship God as He requires. The penalty for worshiping God as the 144,000 direct will be great. The penalty for obeying the laws of Babylon will be even greater! This obvious dilemma is how God establishes the great test of faith that will separate the sheep from the goats. (A wonderful parallel is found in Daniel 3.) Let there be no mistake about it, the Great Tribulation will be a time of wrath for all people, languages and nations.

The Gospel Truth

Remember, God will use the destructive forces of the first four trumpets to literally arrest the attention of all survivors, hoping they will consider His gospel and learn what He wants. In other words, the world must hear the unvarnished truth about God and His authority over man. *God creates this setting to tell the world how He is to be worshiped.* Notice the order of events: God destroys a third of Earth so that the subject of worship becomes a consuming issue. Then, God speaks through His servants, the 144,000. They will explain what God wants. Everyone will hear the truth on this matter. This is why Jesus said the gospel must go to every nation and to every person – as a testimony to all nations – before the end comes. (Matthew 24:14) The testimony of the 144,000 will stand in direct opposition to what the religious leaders of Babylon want to do. The book of Revelation predicts that Babylon will enact laws regarding worship that are contrary to God's will, and regrettably, most of the world will submit to the laws of man rather than obey the law of God. John wrote, **"All inhabitants of the Earth will worship the beast [Babylon] all whose names have not been written in the book of life belonging to the Lamb that was slain from the creation of the world."** (Revelation 13:8, insertion mine)

Chapter 5
The Devil Appears in Person

The first four trumpets will reduce life on Earth to total chaos. The religious coalition that forms in response to God's judgments (Babylon) will make a desperate situation only worse by tormenting people with laws that have severe penalties for disobedience. After a period of about two and a half years, the fifth trumpet judgment occurs. (Revelation 9:1-12) The first four trumpets are curses that are directed at the physical elements of Earth and the remaining three trumpets are curses (or woes) that are directed toward defiant people. (Revelation 9:12) In my opinion, the curse of the fifth trumpet is far worse than the physical destruction caused by the first four trumpets. The fifth trumpet marks the appearing of the Antichrist. The Antichrist is not an ordinary man. The Antichrist is a fallen angel and he will physically appear before the inhabitants of Earth. That ancient serpent, the devil, who deceived Eve in the Garden of Eden, will appear in the clouds with all his angels. Clothed in brilliant light and masquerading as God, the devil will appear in all of the great cities of Earth, one at a time. Daniel 11:45 indicates he will establish a throne in Jerusalem. Many orthodox Jews anticipate the arrival of Messiah and many Palestinians anticipate a Deliverer, so what better place could the devil choose "to initiate a reign of peace on Earth for 1,000 years!" The devil will say many blasphemous things and make outrageous claims in order to deceive the people of Earth. When Satan appears, he will be more resplendent than anything human beings have ever seen and he will claim to be the "Savior of the World." Think about this. When he appears, the world will be in a desperate position and cries of suffering will be everywhere. The father of lies and misery, the enemy of all humanity, will feign sympathy for the terrible human suffering he sees. To make his deception believable, he will perform great signs, such as healing the sick and feeding the hungry. (2 Thessalonians 2:9) Many people will be duped into believing the devil is Almighty God.

Who is the Devil?

According to the Bible, the devil once had an exalted name. His name was Lucifer which means "light bearer." A review of Isaiah 14:12-17 and Ezekiel 28:12-18 reveals that Lucifer was once an anointed cherub in Heaven. Eventually, he became arrogant and self seeking. He became dissatisfied with God's kingdom, God's laws, and the way God was running the universe. Because of hatred for Christ, he recruited one-third of Heaven's angels to join him in rebellion against Christ. Thus, Lucifer is the original "anti-Christ." The Father did everything possible to divert Lucifer's course of action, but the devil would not relent. According to Isaiah 14:12, Lucifer and his angels were cast out of Heaven because of rebellion. Jesus told His disciples, **"I saw Satan fall like lightning from Heaven."** (Luke 10:18)

Angry and embittered by his fallen state, Lucifer focused his wrath on Christ's special handiwork – planet Earth. The devil went to the Garden of Eden and he led Eve to disobey God. Then, Eve seduced Adam and he disobeyed God. The devil did not stop his work there. Cain, the firstborn of Adam and Eve, became a murderer. As time went by, human beings became so defiled by sin that God was grieved that He had even made man! (Genesis 6) Consequently, God washed the Earth clean of sin with a flood of water, sparing just eight people – Noah and his family. The flood may have slowed the devil down for a few years, but Peter tells us the devil is going about like a roaring lion seeking whom he may devour! (1 Peter 5:8,9)

Satan Allowed to Live

Many, many people have asked the question: Why did God allow the devil to live? Why didn't God exterminate Satan and his evil angels right away and spare the universe a great deal of grief? God's ways are perfect and the answer to this question is both simple and profound. Consider the following issues:

1. What message would God have given to the angels if He immediately annihilated every angel that disagreed with Him? If God had destroyed Lucifer as soon as Lucifer sinned, surviving angels would have concluded that God does not tolerate anyone who has ideas that are contrary to His. How could intelligent angels love and trust God if He immediately annihilated His opposition? Should angels love God because God is fair and reasonable, generous and forgiving, or should angels submit to Him because to do otherwise would mean sudden death? If God had killed Lucifer and his followers right away, the remaining angels would have been forced to conclude that God was an omnipotent bully ruling over the universe.

2. God has infinite wisdom and He foreknew that sin needed time to mature so that all the universe could see the deadly and horrible consequences of sin. By allowing the devil and his angels to live for a few thousand years, the universe would have two governments to study – one in Heaven (free of sin) and one on Earth (full of sin). The presence of two governments will ultimately prove that God's laws and principles of government are best – not because He claims they are best – but because God's ways have been demonstrated to be best.

3. God gives the power of choice to each created being. His subjects do not have to obey Him, love Him, or respond to His goodness or generosity. Lucifer and his angels exercised their power of choice by choosing to rebel against God. Adam and Eve were given the power of choice and they chose to disobey God. For 6,000 years, sin has contaminated Earth. Time has proven that the quality of life suffers in proportion to our rebellion against the laws of God. True, sin may offer pleasure and excitement for a short time, but it always extracts a price that is far greater than the brief high of a cheap thrill. Sin takes us farther than we want to go, and sin costs us more than we want to pay. No matter how well Satan disguises sin, **"the wages of sin is death."** (Romans 6:23)

4. God foreknew the consequences of allowing Satan and his angels to live. Yet, at great expense to Himself, God provided a plan to save everyone who would live on Earth. He loved the people of the world so much that He gave us His only Son's life. Jesus was willing to come and die in man's place so the penalty for sin would be paid! God Himself has paid a much greater price for the existence of sin than any human being will ever know! Incidently, a plan of salvation was not offered to Lucifer and his angels because they willfully committed the unpardonable sin. (Matthew 12:31,32)

When these four items are brought together, we discover why God did not immediately destroy Lucifer and his followers. The conflict between Christ and Lucifer has been in progress on Earth for 6,000 years. Today, Christ and Satan are still striving to win the affections of people. This struggle will come to a dramatic end during the Great Tribulation.

Out of the Bottomless Pit

Revelation predicts that the devil will enter the realm of our human senses and he will appear physically before our eyes. Revelation 9 tells us the devil is an angel king that will come up out of the abyss (or bottomless pit, KJV)! To appreciate this prediction and the meaning of John's language, we need to review a little ancient history.

People thought Earth was flat, much like a large plate or basin in Bible times. Since they had limited knowledge about the law of gravity, it seemed logical to the ancients that Earth was made like a basin – otherwise the great seas would "drain away." Because Earth was believed to be flat, the ancients concluded a bottomless pit could be created if a person dug a hole all the way through the "basin." Without a bottom, a person could fall through the "bottomless pit" and never be seen again. The ancients also believed the "fires of hell" burned underneath the basin of Earth and volcanos were enormous chimneys that proved the presence of underground fires. When we understand John's view of the physical world at the time he lived, it helps us understand why God used this type of imagery in the book of Revelation.

The transliteration of the Greek word *abussos* into English is "abyss." Whether it is called "bottomless pit" (KJV) or "abyss" (NIV), the idea is the same. In ancient times, the "bottomless pit" represented a poorly defined source or origin of mythological monsters and demons. The ancients believed surreal creatures lived "under the basin" of Earth and when the creatures escaped, they came up through caves or holes which had no bottom or end to them. When God revealed last day events to John in A.D. 95, God used geographical ideas that were familiar to John. For example, John saw the devil and his angels ascend from a bottomless pit and John refers to this event in several places in the book of Revelation. By putting on John's sandals and considering the mind set of his day, we can understand God's use of imagery. Many people are surprised to learn that Revelation predicts the physical appearance of Satan on Earth before Jesus returns! However, Revelation not only tells us when, but it also tells us why!

The Fifth Trumpet

"The fifth angel sounded his trumpet, and I saw a star that had fallen from the sky to the Earth. The star was given the key to the shaft of the Abyss. When he opened the Abyss, smoke rose from it like the smoke from a gigantic furnace. The sun and sky were darkened by the smoke from the Abyss. And out of the smoke locusts came down upon the earth and were given power like that of scorpions of the earth. They were told not to harm the grass of the earth or any plant or tree, but only those people who did not have the seal of God on their foreheads. They were not given power to kill them, but only to torture them for five months. And the agony they suffered was like that of the sting of a scorpion when it strikes a man. During those days men will seek death, but will not find it; they will long to die, but death will elude them. . . . They [the locusts] had as king

over them the angel of the Abyss, whose name in Hebrew is Abaddon, and in Greek, Apollyon. " (Revelation
9:1-6, 11, insertion mine)

God does not permit the devil to escape from his prison in the
abyss (the spirit world) until the sounding of the fifth trumpet.
At an appointed time, the bottomless pit will be "unlocked" and
the devil and his angels will be allowed to come out of the
spirit realm and be visible to the people of Earth. God illus-
trated the appearing of the devil and his angels to John as a
great swarm of locusts coming up out of the Earth. From a
distance, several hundred million angels would look like a
dense swarm of locusts. The swarm that John saw in vision
was so great that he says it darkened the Sun! As the swarm
came closer to him, John saw that the locusts actually looked
like riders on horses. Leading the swarm was the angel king
from the abyss whose name in Hebrew is Abaddon and in
Greek, Apollyon. Both names mean the same thing: "De-
stroyer." The imagery and language used in Revelation 9:1-11
is similar to language used five hundred years earlier in Joel
2:1-11 where the prophet describes the appearing of the Lord
and His angels as a great swarm of locusts prepared for battle.
God permits the devil and his angels to physically appear on
Earth after a majority of the world has heard and rejected the
truth about the worship God requires. Notice Paul's words:
**"They [the majority of people] perish because they refused
to love the truth and so be saved. For this reason God
sends them a powerful delusion so that they will believe
the lie and so that all will be condemned who have not
believed the truth but have delighted in wickedness."**
(2 Thessalonians 2:10-12) The first key point in this verse is
defiance. Paul says "they refused" to obey God's truth and be
saved. Why will they reject God's truth? **"The sinful mind is
hostile to God. It does not submit to God's law, nor can
it do so. Those controlled by the sinful nature cannot
please God."** (Romans 8:7,8) Therefore, when a majority of
people reject God's last offer of salvation, He sends them a
powerful deception. God releases the devil from the abyss and

He empowers the devil to rule over people who refuse to recognize His sovereign authority. This is an interesting point about the Great Tribulation: Each person *will worship* one of two masters.

Three important elements are revealed when God releases Satan and his angels from the bottomless pit. First, Satan will come with a cloud of angels (like a swarm of locusts). These demons will be clothed with brilliant light. Remember, the devil himself will be a magnificent being of dazzling light. (2 Corinthians 11:14) Although Satan will do his utmost to imitate the Second Coming, God limits the devil's deception. When Jesus appears at the Second Coming, Jesus will not touch Earth. The saints will be caught up *in the air* to meet Jesus and He will take them to Heaven where they will spend 1,000 years. (1 Thessalonians 4:15-18; John 14:1-3; Revelation 21:2) However, Satan will come down out of the sky and he will walk upon Earth in various places. This is why Jesus warned, **"At that time if anyone says to you, 'Look, here is the Christ!' or, 'There he is!' do not believe it. . . . So if anyone tells you, 'There he is, out in the desert,' do not go out; or, 'Here he is, in the inner rooms,' do not believe it. For as lightning that comes from the east is visible even in the west, so will be the coming of the Son of Man."** (Matthew 24:23, 26,27)

Second, God does not allow Satan to physically appear on Earth until a majority of the world has rejected the gospel. I believe that this will occur in about a two and a half year period. During this period of time, the 144,000 will proclaim the truth about worshiping God so that everyone on Earth can make an informed decision. The result will be simple. People will either submit to God's law or rebel against it. When God sees that a majority of Earth's population intends to rebel against His gospel, He allows the devil to appear. God has a very wise purpose for doing this. The physical appearing of the devil will force the people of Earth into one of two groups: people who worship God out of choice and people who worship the devil out of force. In a final effort to bring rebellious human beings to their senses, God will empower the 144,000 to proclaim a special message throughout the Earth. This message is so inflammatory that most – if not all – of the 144,000 will become martyrs for preaching it! The message is this: **". . .If anyone worships [obeys] the beast [the devil from the abyss] and his image [his one world church] and receives his mark [tattoo] on the forehead or on the hand, he, too, will drink of the wine of God's fury, which has been poured full strength into the cup of his wrath. He will be tormented with burning sulfur in the presence of the holy angels and of the Lamb."** (Revelation 14:9,10, insertion mine) Since a majority of the world will think the devil is God, speaking against "God" like this will be considered utterly derogatory and blasphemous and the 144,000 will be horribly persecuted for their testimony!

The third reason God allows the devil to physically appear is that God wants people of the world to get a "close up" view of the demon they are following. The issue of worship will be completely resolved after the devil arrives. The devil will demand worship, and through his lieutenants, he will clearly explain what men and women must do. God continues to do no less through His servants, the 144,000. The saints will submit to God's law. The wicked will submit to the law of the devil. This is the vortex surrounding the decision that all humans will face. Every person will exercise his or her power of choice and God will seal every decision.

Five Months of Torture

According to Revelation 9:3-6, after Satan and his evil angels appear, they will have five months to torment the wicked. This may seem strange at first, but God does not let the devil hurt His saints "with the sting of a scorpion's tail." The devil will inflict this torture on the nonreligious wicked in order to subdue them. The devil will not hurt those who believe he is God, either. Instead, he will hurt people who have not made a decision to join with his forces or with God's saints. Just what the torment is and how it is inflicted is not clear from Scripture. However, we do know the torment will hurt like a scorpion's sting (which is awful). The people who suffer this affliction will long to die, but the devil's sting is not fatal. God allows the devil to torment "undecided" people with scorpion-like pain because God's offer of salvation is still open. Everyone that the devil harms can be delivered from agony *if* he or she will turn from rebellion and worship the Lord. (See Numbers 21:6-9 for a parallel story.) Remember, God will do everything possible during the Great Tribulation to save as many sinners as possible!

An Angel of Light That Works Miracles

When Satan appears, his radiant countenance will dazzle the people of Earth. Millions will eagerly believe his claims that he is God because of his appearance alone. Paul says, **". . . for Satan himself masquerades as an angel of light."** (2 Corinthians 11:14) Revelation says the wicked will be awestruck when they actually see the devil! **". . . The inhabitants of the Earth whose names have not been written in the book of life from the creation of the world will be *astonished* when they see the beast . . . ."** (Revelation 17:8, italics mine.)

Satan's first work after appearing "in the flesh" as a brilliant God-man will be to convince the world that he is divine – that he is actually who he claims to be. Paul warns, **"Don't let anyone deceive you in any way, for that day (the second coming) will not come until the rebellion occurs and the man of lawlessness is revealed, the man doomed to destruction. He opposes and exalts himself over everything that is called God or is worshiped, and even sets himself up in God's temple, proclaiming himself to be God. . . . The coming of the lawless one will be in accordance with the work of Satan displayed in all kinds of counterfeit miracles, signs and wonders, and in every sort of evil that deceives those who are perishing. They perish because they refused to love the truth and so be saved."** (2 Thessalonians 2:3,4,9,10)

The Greatest Deception of All

To convince people that he is God, Satan will use one miracle above all others – he will actually call fire down out of Heaven at will! This "proof of divinity" will secure his deception. Because the 144,000 will not have this specific miracle working power, the devil will eclipse their power and bring their ministry to an end. (Revelation 11:7) John says, **"And he performed great and miraculous signs, even causing fire to come down from heaven to Earth in full view of men. Because of the signs he was given power to do on behalf of the first beast, he deceived the inhabitants of the Earth . . . ."** (Revelation 13:13,14) Remember, the appearing of the devil is "a powerful delusion" sent from God. The devil is granted power to call fire down from Heaven because God is bringing the offer of salvation to an end. Prior to the devil's appearing, God put forth the clearest evidences of truth before the human race through the testimony of His 144,000 servants. God wants people to worship Him on the basis of "Spirit and truth," not miracles! (John 4:23) Therefore, God reduces the ministry and power of His servants while increasing the deceptive powers of the Antichrist.

John describes the appearing of the devil as a "lamb-like" beast. (Revelation 13:11) The intended contrast is obvious. Depending on the Bible translation, Revelation refers to Jesus as the "Lamb" 30 or more times. John describes Satan as a "lamb-like" beast because the devil masquerades as Jesus. John warns that Satan will make every effort to deceive the world into believing that he is worthy of worship. When Satan appears, every quadrant of Earth will have experienced massive destruction. Extreme suffering will be everywhere. Earth's skies will have been dark for a long time, and millions of people (perhaps billions) will have grown deathly ill from famine. The death toll will be numberless, and millions of people will die every day from plague and disease. People will be filled with despair, and religious leaders will constantly reprimand sinners, telling them to repent and worship God so that His wrath will subside. Religious persecution and intolerance will be everywhere because Babylon (the coalition of religious leaders) will be determined to appease God at any cost. (What other option do they have?) Foremost in all people's minds will be the question, "What more can we do to appease God so that He will end our suffering?"

In the midst of this hellish nightmare, the devil suddenly appears. Satan uses incredible displays of signs and wonders to deceive, if possible, the very elect. (Matthew 24:24-25) His purpose has always been to destroy this world because it is the handiwork of Christ. When Satan's day of opportunity comes, it will be the perfect moment for him to fulfill this ambition. The devil will capitalize on the rebellious hearts of the wicked. He will lead the majority of the world away from hearing and believing the truth preached by God's servants, the 144,000. Because of the miracles that he has power to do, the devil will deceive or destroy everyone but the saints. After he gains control of Earth's nations, he will command the people of the world to worship "the image" or die! Revelation 13:15 says, **"He, [Satan] . . . caused all who refused to worship the image to be killed."**

The Image of the Beast

What is the *image* of the beast? Who does the beast represent? The beast from the sea in Revelation 13:1-8 represents Babylon. The seven heads represent the seven religions of the world and the ten horns represent ten kings who will play a strategic role near the end of the world. The *image* of Babylon will be a consolidation of the world's diverse religions and nations into one global church/state. When the majority of Catholics, Jews, Protestants, Moslems, Hindus and all others believe that Satan is actually God, they will be willing to do whatever he demands. Can a human being give too much or do too much for God? The devil will demand that all religions must be dissolved into one religion. Think about this for a moment. If God were physically on Earth to establish His eternal kingdom, how many different churches could He allow? How many views of God are possible when God is physically among men to reveal what is truth? The establishment of an "image" is the establishment of a likeness of Babylon. In short, the devil will form a new composite religion and he will require everyone to leave his old religion behind. His new religion will be designed to dissolve the antagonistic differences between Moslems, Jews, Hindus, Catholics, Protestants, etc. This new church or religion will have a special benefit. All who join it will receive permission to buy and sell. The members of the devil's kingdom will have access to the necessities of life (food, water, medicine, etc.) which the devil's forces will control. In other words, citizens of the devil's kingdom will be able to buy and sell because they will receive a mark or tattoo showing that they belong to the "One True Church." The saints, on the other hand, will be cut off from all necessities of life. It's just as well, for they would rather die than submit to the demands of the devil. The wicked will volunteer to receive the mark of the beast, justifying that it is a small price to pay for survival. Meanwhile, the saints will be fed and cared for by angels sent from God.

Chapter 6
Worship the Beast or Die

A Time of Testing

Someone has said that truth can be stranger than fiction. If this is true, then here is a truth that could be stranger than fiction: *The Bible predicts the final generation will face a life and death controversy over the question of worship.* Many people think worship means "going to church," but worship involves far more than going to a worship service. Worship means submission and obedience to God – as in fulfilling a divine obligation or duty out of love for God. A terrible controversy over worship will occur during the Great Tribulation because salvation will come through the worship of Jesus Christ (John 5:23,24) and condemnation will come through the worship of the Antichrist. (Revelation 14:9,10)

When Abel sacrificed the *required* lamb, he worshiped God. When Cain offered fruit to God, he did not worship God – he offended God because he did not do what God commanded. Often, worship is considered a casual matter. When and how (or if) an individual worships is a personal matter for the most part. Worship is sometimes described as a celebration service or meditation. Worship is regarded as an expression of devotion to God and each religious body is free to worship according to what it believes is God's will. When the Great Tribulation begins, the topic of worship will suddenly change from that of personal taste to that of corporate responsibility. Suddenly, the issue of how God is to be worshiped will be debated because people will assume that they can appease God's wrath by worshiping Him properly. According to Revelation, the people of Earth will become sharply divided over the worship of God during the Great Tribulation. Ultimately, there will be two camps of worshipers, one will worship the Lamb (the sheep) and the other will worship the lamb-like beast (the goats).

The Bible predicts the first four trumpet judgments of God will kill 25% of the world's population. (Revelation 6:8) As a result, despair, anxiety and depression will be pandemic. In this awful and desperate setting, consider the simplicity of these words: **"*All inhabitants* of the Earth will *worship* the beast [Babylon] – all whose names have not been written in the book of life belonging to the Lamb that was slain from the creation of the world."** (Revelation 13:8, insertion and italics mine) The words "all inhabitants of the Earth" are inclusive. The *only* people who will refuse to worship the beast will be the saints. It is hard to believe that millions of people will rebel against God and submit to the authority of Babylon, but it is true. When the devil appears on Earth, he will consolidate the diversity of Babylon's religions into a one world church/state. At that time, wicked people rebelling against both God and the devil will have no choice but to worship the devil or die. Notice the horrible consequences that will befall people who worship the devil: **"If anyone worships the [lamb-like] beast and his image and receives his mark on the forehead or on the hand, he, too, will drink of the wine of God's fury, which has been poured full strength into the cup of his wrath. He will be tormented with burning sulfur in the presence of the holy angels and of the Lamb."** (Revelation 14:9,10, insertion mine) This verse contains one of the most solemn warnings found in the entire Bible. God means what He says and we can be sure that death by burning sulfur will not be a pleasant experience.

The other side of the controversy will have deadly consequences also. Many saints will be tortured and killed by the devil's forces for refusing to worship the beast! **". . . He** [the lamb-like beast] **ordered them to set up an image in honor of the beast who was wounded by the sword and yet lived. He was given power to give breath to the image of the first beast, so that it could speak and cause all who refused to worship the image to be killed."** (Revelation 13:14,15, insertion mine)

Revelation says a huge number of saints will be killed during the Great Tribulation: **"When he [the Lamb] opened the fifth seal, I saw under the altar the souls of those who had been slain because of the word of God and the testimony they had maintained. They called out in a loud voice, 'How long, Sovereign Lord, holy and true, until you judge the inhabitants of the earth and avenge our blood?' "** (Revelation 6:9,10) When the devil gains control of Earth, he will not tolerate rebellion against his authority. The devil will be more cruel and ruthless than Hitler. Millions will be martyred. John writes, **"This calls for patient endurance on the part of the saints who obey God's commandments and remain faithful to Jesus."** (Revelation 14:12) There is a profound point about martyrdom which you must know. God will give a martyr's faith to everyone facing a martyr's death. Jesus said, **". . . And surely I am with you always, to the very end of the age."** (Matthew 28:20) **"All this I have told you so that you will not go astray. They will put you out of the synagogue; in fact, a time is coming when anyone who kills you will think he is offering a service to God. They will do such things because they have not known the Father or me."** (John 16:1-3)

While we are considering the coming martyrdom of saints, consider God's wrath upon those who kill His saints: **"The third angel poured out his bowl on the rivers and springs of water, and they became blood. Then I heard the angel in charge of the waters say: 'You are just in these judgments, you who are and who were, the Holy One, because you have so judged; for they have shed the blood of your saints and prophets, and you have given them blood to drink as they deserve.' "** (Revelation 16:4-6) This verse describes the third bowl which occurs during the seven last plagues (God's destructive wrath). God pours the third bowl of His wrath – full strength – upon those people who participated in killing His saints during the Great Tribulation. God avenges the innocent blood of His saints by giving these bloodthirsty people blood to drink. These evil people will suffer

horribly for their crimes against humanity. In addition to this
horrible suffering, their lives will be sustained so that they
might perish in burning sulfur. The wrath of God is far worse
than anything man can do. Jesus warned, **"But I will show
you whom you should fear: Fear him who, after the
killing of the body, has power to throw you into hell.
Yes, I tell you, fear him."** (Luke 12:5)

Powerful Irony

When God's judgments begin, God's servants, the 144,000, will
tell a dazed and reeling world that God is angry because there
is no respect for His laws or His authority. They will remind
everyone that God's Ten Commandments are ten demands the
Creator imposes on all creation. Specifically, the fourth commandment requires the cessation of work on God's seventh day
Sabbath. Ironically, the leaders of the religious coalition will
say the same thing! The problem will be that Babylon's Sabbath and God's Sabbath will be two different days! This dispar-
ity will make the issue of "worship" very interesting. The
religious leaders of Babylon will say with a united voice that
God has sent judgments upon mankind because Earth's inhabitants have sinned greatly and have become degenerate. They
will call for immediate action to appease God. The religious
leaders of Babylon will *sincerely* demand laws from their
legislators requiring everyone to honor and worship the God of
Heaven. Hindu and Buddhist leaders will solve the worship
problem by imposing their views of worship upon their nations.
Moslem leaders will impose their views upon their nations.
Jewish rabbis, Catholic priests and Protestant clergy will all
do the same.

A Holy Day Mystery

God has clearly expressed in the Bible how His subjects are to
worship Him. This is not a matter left to human design, for if it
was, humans would have greater authority than God. *The one
dictating the time and manner of worship has highest authority.* Unfortunately, the devil has obscured God's truth about
worship and implemented false religion around the world.

During the end time, Babylon will face a peculiar problem. Each religious system in Babylon will demand that God be worshiped in a variety of ways. For example, Moslems regard Friday as a holy day, Jews regard Saturday as a holy day and Christians regard Sunday as a holy day! So, each religion will ask its lawmakers to enact laws exalting *their* day of worship. The Bible says that when people obey the laws of Babylon, they will be worshiping the devil because the devil is the power within Babylon. **"Men worshiped the dragon** [devil] **because he had given authority to the beast** [Babylon]**, and they also worshiped the beast** [Babylon] **and asked, "Who is like the beast** [Babylon]**? Who can make war** [rebel] **against him?"** (Revelation 13:4)

The story of Cain and Abel is recorded in the Bible because it illustrates the primary difference between true worship and false worship. Both men built altars. Abel worshiped God by obediently sacrificing a lamb according to God's instruction. Cain refused to obey God. Instead, he chose to do what he thought was best. In effect, Cain presumed to tell his Creator how He would be worshiped. By doing this, Cain insulted God and God rejected Cain's offering. (Genesis 4:1-16)

Cain's rebellious heart led to Cain's rejection. Because of rejection, Cain became violently angry and killed his brother. John warns, **"Do not be like Cain, who belonged to the evil one and murdered his brother. And why did he murder him? Because his own actions were evil and his brother's were righteous. Do not be surprised, my brothers, if the world hates you."** (1 John 3:12,13) John says Cain's "act of worship" was evil! In fact, God considered it a blasphemous act because Cain assumed the prerogatives that belong only to God. Cain thought he could tell God how He should be worshiped! Look at this from God's perspective for a moment. If a created being can tell his Creator how or when He is to be worshiped, then the created being is greater than his Creator. Remember, *the one dictating the time and manner of worship has highest authority.*

The crux of the matter is this: God accepts our worship if we worship Him in Spirit and in truth; that is, if we honestly worship God according to all that we know to be right and true. At the present time, many people worship God thinking they are doing the right thing, when in reality they are not worshiping God as He commands. God kindly winks at our ignorance. However, during the Great Tribulation, God has determined that the whole world must be informed about worship. This is why worship will become the central issue during the Great Tribulation. The 144,000 will preach the gospel of Jesus Christ to every nation, kindred, and tongue as a testimony to all nations (Matthew 24:14) and the gospel of Jesus Christ contains specific information about the worship of Jesus. The 144,000 will proclaim "**. . . Fear God and give him glory, because the hour of his judgment has come. Worship him who made the Heavens, the Earth, the sea and the springs of water.**" (Revelation 14:7) The 144,000 will present the first message which will be "fear God" and "worship the Creator" because a vast majority of the world's population does neither. God understands Earth's spiritual darkness and He has winked at our ignorance for a long time, but overnight, He will remove the darkness that covers the subject of worship *by displaying His wrath*. After Jesus tears the Earth up with a display of awesome power, He will have everyone's attention. Then, He will send His servants throughout the world and with Holy Spirit power, they will expel the darkness that Satan has placed around the subject of worshiping God on His holy Sabbath, the seventh day of the week. The honest in heart within every religion will hear the call to worship Jesus and they will receive Christ as their Savior and worship Jesus according to our Creator's demands.

Worship the Creator

This may come as a surprise, but 95% of the references about God in the Bible refer to Jesus. The Father rarely speaks in the Bible. Jesus is the God of the Old Testament and He is the God of the New Testament. (Isaiah 45; John 5:39,40; 8:58) Jesus is the Creator of Heaven and Earth. (John 1:1-14;

Colossians 1:16-19; Hebrews 1:1-3) These facts are presented because Jesus is not a lesser God than the Father as many suppose. (John 5:23; Colossians 2:9) Jesus is fully God and He did not leave worship to human design. Jesus clearly explains in the Ten Commandments how *He* is to be worshiped. Carefully review His first four commands. They are found in Exodus 20:3-11:

Commandment 1. "You shall have no other gods before me."

Commandment 2. "You shall not make for yourself an idol in the form of anything in heaven above or on the Earth beneath or in the waters below. You shall not bow down to them or worship them; for I, the Lord your God, am a jealous God, punishing the children for the sin of the fathers to the third and fourth generation of those who hate me, but showing love to thousands who love me and keep my commandments."

Commandment 3. "You shall not misuse the name of the Lord your God, for the Lord will not hold anyone guiltless who misuses his name."

Commandment 4. "Remember the Sabbath day by keeping it holy. Six days you shall labor and do all your work, but the seventh day is a Sabbath to the Lord your God. On it you shall not do any work, neither you, nor your son or daughter, nor your manservant or maidservant, nor your animals, nor the alien within your gates. For in six days the Lord made the heavens and the Earth, the sea, and all that is in them, but he rested on the seventh day. Therefore the Lord blessed the Sabbath day and made it holy."

These four commandments outline the basics of worship. They explain the reverence and respect due our Creator. We are not to obey or reverence any other God. We are not to create an idol and bow down before it. We are not to use or represent the name of God in a careless way. And, we are to observe the *seventh day of the week* as a memorial to our Creator and our Redeemer by resting from our labors on Saturday, just as He rested from His.

Confrontational Issue

When confronted with the demands of the fourth commandment, most Christians argue that the seventh day Sabbath was abolished or nailed to the cross. The implication is that when Jesus came to Earth, He did away with the Ten Commandments, including the "Sabbath of the Jews." The Bible disagrees. The fourth commandment does not grant ownership of the Sabbath to the Jews. Rather, it says the "**the seventh day is a Sabbath to the Lord your God.**" The Bible indicates the seventh day was made holy long before there was any Jew on Earth! In fact, the seventh day Sabbath was created and set apart as a special day at Creation. When properly understood, the beauty of God's Sabbath shines from Creation's week revealing a special gift that Jesus gave to mankind. Think of it – God's Sabbath was the first full day of life for Adam and Eve! Jesus created the Sabbath, He made it holy at Creation and He gave it to man: **"Thus the heavens and the earth were completed in all their vast array. By the seventh day God had finished the work he had been doing; so on the seventh day he rested from all his work. And God blessed the seventh day and made it holy, because on it he rested from all the work of creating that he had done."** (Genesis 2:1-3) Four thousand years later Jesus said, **". . . The Sabbath was made for man, not man for the Sabbath, so the Son of Man is Lord even of the Sabbath."** (Mark 2:27,28)

If the topic of the seventh day Sabbath is a controversial subject in the best of times, what will it be during the worst of times? God's seventh day Sabbath will prove to be highly controversial during the Great Tribulation for three reasons: First, our carnal nature is inherently opposed to obeying God's law: **"The sinful mind is hostile to God. It does not submit to God's law, nor can it do so."** (Romans 8:7) Second, few people have enough time to get everything done that needs to be done throughout the week. Asking most people to "give up" 24 hours each week to worship God seems to be asking too much. Last, God's Sabbath has a very determined adversary. The devil has made sure that Saturday observance puts a person at odds with the social and religious orders of life. The observance of Sabbath interrupts every aspect of life. This is why God created the Sabbath in the first place. Jesus wanted to interrupt man's relentless pursuit for money and pleasure every week with a whole day of rest. Because Jesus knew that mankind would stray from His Sabbath, God bound the observance of His Sabbath upon mankind with the authority of law. When these factors are added together, it is easy to see why most of the world prefers to worship God according to their own ideas. They believe that, "Jesus wants too much."

The Ten Commandments are divided into two groups, and therefore, they were written on two tablets of stone. (Exodus 34:29) The first four commandments deal with man's relationship to God, and the last six deal with man's relationship to his neighbor. Actually, the Ten Commandments summarize the two essential laws of life. Jesus summarized them saying, "... 'Love the Lord your God with all your heart and with all your soul and with all your mind.' This is the first and greatest commandment. And the second is like it: 'Love your neighbor as yourself.' All the Law and the Prophets hang on these two commandments."** (Matthew 22:37-40; Jesus quotes from Deuteronomy 6:5; Leviticus 19:18.)

Love and faith are the foundation of salvation. Love makes submission a joy, and faith (believing God's Word) is the basis for obedience. The two "love" commandments that Jesus mentioned are defined by the Ten Commandments. *The meaning of love is not left to human definition.* Unfortunately, the word "love" today, commonly means sex, lust or passion. What a perversion! According to Jesus, true love is a high and holy principle that produces joyful obedience! **"Whoever has my commands and obeys them, he is the one who loves me. He who loves me will be loved by my Father, and I too**

will love him and show myself to him. . . . If anyone
loves me, he will obey my teaching. . . . He who does not
love me will not obey my teaching . . . ." (John 14:21-24)

As we would expect, Satan has effectively led the human race
to diminish the importance of the Ten Commandments. The
devil has especially tried to hide the requirement of the fourth
commandment which contains instruction on *how* to worship
and *when* to worship our Creator. Satan's purpose for doing
this is simple. Bible history confirms that when people ignore
the Sabbath of their Creator, they also forget their Creator.
When people forget their Creator, they soon create false gods
that are compatible with the carnal nature because mankind
inherently needs something to exalt and worship. God created
this desire within us. Satan has enjoyed enormous success
displacing our Creator with false gods. Many people have no
idea that God demands rest on the seventh day of the week.
God has winked at man's ignorance and darkness on this
subject for a very long time. This is not God's loss; it is man's
loss because the Sabbath was created for man by an all knowing Creator! Every violation of God's law diminishes the quality of life that God wants for His children. Degeneracy is the
result of rebellion and separation from the renewing power of
God. If a person does not love and obey his or her Creator, he
or she has broken the first commandment because that person
will love and obey another god. **"Who foretold this long ago,
who declared it from the distant past? Was it not I, the
Lord? And there is no God apart from me, a righteous
God and a Savior; there is none but me. Turn to me and
be saved, all you ends of the earth; for I am God, and
there is no other."** (Isaiah 45:21,22)

Jesus will use the first four trumpets to strip away our finan-
cial security and our foolish attraction for gods of wood, metal,
stone, pleasure, materialism and self reliance. A $75,000
Mercedes will be of no value without fuel or roads on which to
drive. A $500,000 house will be worthless if it is reduced to a
pile of rubble by the first global earthquake. God is about to
awaken people all over the world. Then everyone will get a

chance to see how great our corporate rebellion is against Him. This rebellion will center on the issue of worship, specifically on the observance of our Creator's Sabbath.

Jesus is Almighty God

Knowledge of an omnipotent and angry God will explode all over the Earth during the Great Tribulation! No one will be able to deny God's wrath. God's silence with the transgression of His law will end and all creation will know that He sits enthroned in Heaven. He is Almighty God. He is Sovereign over Heaven and Earth and He will send a clarion call throughout the Earth to worship Him on His holy day – Saturday, the seventh day of the week. The call to worship Him as He dictates will separate the sheep from the goats.

Consider these three points:

1. God declared the seventh day of the week holy at Creation because He rested on the seventh day to commemorate His creation of this world! The word *holy* means "set apart." God made the seventh day uniquely different from the other six days at Creation – not at Mount Sinai! It was God who set the seventh day apart from the others. (Genesis 2:2,3)

2. Because God foreknew that Satan would successfully lead the world to forget or deny the holiness of the seventh day Sabbath, the fourth commandment begins with the word "Remember." (Exodus 20:8)

3. Contrary to what religious leaders say, God Himself declared the seventh day of the week to be holy and He has not rescinded this declaration. *All* other days, according to God, are for work and common activities. (Exodus 20:9)

Were the Ten Commandments Abolished?

If you ask most Christians about the Ten Commandments, they will agree that nine of the ten are good. (The implication, of course, is that one is bad.) They will agree that it is wrong to steal, kill another human being, commit adultery, use God's name in vain or worship idols. In fact, much of the Christian world will tell you that nine of the Ten Commandments benefit society. But when you ask questions about the fourth commandment, you will hear how the Ten Commandments were nailed to the cross and are no longer binding upon humanity. Why this contradiction?

For centuries, Catholic and Protestant clerics have said the Ten Commandments were nailed to the cross. This explains why most Christians today see no reason to be concerned about the demands of the fourth commandment. If we could reason from cause to effect, we would immediately recognize that our world finds itself in a dismal state today singularly due to lawlessness. Parents have not taught their children the importance of man's laws, not to mention God's higher laws. When the importance of law and obedience is neglected in childhood, moral absolutes evaporate and another law, the law of the jungle, prevails. In the jungle of evil, the strongest players rule by deceit or whim (i.e., machine gun, brute force, etc.). The United States has incarcerated more people than any other developed nation. Why is this? When the beauty and necessity of law is ignored in childhood, lawlessness takes over. Safety, virtue and nobility of character disappear when lawlessness rules. Painful suffering, broken relationships, greed, drugs, sexual depravity and needless deaths are evidences of lawlessness. When the beacon of moral law declines, decadence, chaos and misery overtakes society. This cause to effect progression explains why God has had to destroy civilizations from time to time. When the cup of iniquity becomes full, total destruction is the *only* solution.

Law and Grace

Many people are confused about the close harmony that exists between God's law and God's grace, even though we routinely apply these concepts in our lives. Law and grace are brother and sister – they are inseparably related. In fact, they cannot exist without each other. We need grace because law is present. If God had no law, God's grace would not be necessary! Paul and John say that when there is no law, there is no sin! (See Romans 4:15 and 1 John 3:4-6.) However, grace does not lessen the obedience that laws demand either! (Romans 3:31)

If a judge pardons a speeding ticket, does this act of "grace" release the offender from the requirement to obey the speed limit in the future? Not at all. In this example, the law remains intact and grace provides forgiveness to the offender for that one offense. In practice, the harmony between law and grace is easy to understand. For example, when two people are united in love, there are certain nonnegotiable rules the couple must follow if they are to maintain fidelity within the relationship. Faithfulness is one nonnegotiable rule. So it is with our Creator. If we love Him, we have to abide by His nonnegotiable rules, not for the purpose of salvation, but to maintain that all important relationship with Him. **"Can two walk together, except they be agreed?"** (Amos 3:3, KJV) A person cannot have a relationship with God without obeying Him. God is not our equal. **"When Abram was ninety-nine years old, the Lord** [Jesus] **appeared to him and said, 'I am God Almighty; walk before me and be blameless.'"** (Genesis 17:1, insertion mine) Jesus is Sovereign God of the Universe. Jesus said, **"If you love me, you will obey what I command. . . . You are my friends if you do what I command."** (John 14:15; 15:14)

The world will soon hear the message that God's Ten Commandments are nonnegotiable. Religious leaders have declared God's commandments void, and many people, including Christians, are ignorant of God's laws. However, Jesus will remove this ignorance with a display of powerful judgments and the preaching of the 144,000. God's judgments are coming on the world because a majority of the world's population do not honor the other nine commandments! God is justifiably angry with humankind. He owns a planet that is constantly at war. Humankind has little love or trust for one another. Instead, they prefer to kill, cheat, lie, commit idolatry and adultery, and steal from each other. On top of this, few people on this planet really love God enough to do what He commands. Each sin adds to the cup and when the cup spills over, God acts. God's patience with sin has a limit.

Let me be clear, obedience does not bring salvation, for salvation is not based on a perfection obtained through obedience. Salvation is based on faith. Faith in God is expressed by our "willingness" to obey Him. Obeying God's laws are for our benefit, not His. Think about it. Why would anyone reject the idea of having the seventh day set aside to rest each week? Disobeying God's laws always reduces the quality of life. If we live in harmony with God's laws, we can live life to the fullest, as God created life to be lived. If we ignore God's laws, death and misery are the end result. If we live according to God's laws, we can enjoy the pursuit of happiness and the fullness of life that He wants us to have. If we ignore them, the consequences are self-evident. Magazines and newspapers print the horrible results every day.

A Test of Faith

God has thoughtfully designed a final exam for Earth. He will grant Satan and his forces complete control of the world's religious and political systems for a short time. Individuals who love God above all else will, on pain of imprisonment, torture and death, obey His law! A watching universe will ·clearly see who would rather die than obey the devil. The sheep will be separated from the goats. Consider this contest carefully. Circumstances will be so desperate during the Great Tribulation that obeying the Ten Commandments will be impossible, except through faith! In other words, the only way a person will be able to obey Jesus and keep His commandments will be through faith in God's promises. This is why John identified the remnant of God's people as follows: **"Then the dragon [the devil] was enraged at the woman and went off to make war against the rest of her offspring – those who obey God's commandments and hold to the testimony of Jesus."** (Revelation 12:17)

Are There Reasons to Worship on Sunday?

During the Great Tribulation, the United States (and many other nations that have a Christian majority) will make and enforce laws regarding the sacredness of Sunday, even though there is not a hint of a command in the Bible to worship God on Sunday. Sunday is not, nor has it ever been, God's day of worship. Many God-fearing people mistakenly believe that Sunday is the Lord's day. Eloquent scholars have produced volumes offering sophisticated logic to whitewash the error, but *the Bible does not teach that Sunday replaced Sabbath as God's day of worship after Jesus died on the cross.* There are eight texts in the New Testament that mention the first day of the week. Therefore, direct biblical support for the sacredness of Sunday has to come from these eight verses. Here are the texts:

Matthew 28:1	Mark 16:2
Mark 16:9	Luke 24:1
John 20:1	John 20:19
Acts 20:7	1 Corinthians 16:2

The texts in Matthew, Mark, Luke and John state Jesus was resurrected on the first day of the week – a well accepted fact. However, none of these texts mention anything about the sacredness of Sunday. In fact, Luke 23:56 points out that a group of women did not prepare the Lord's body for burial late Friday afternoon, but instead rested on the Sabbath "according to the commandment." Their behavior indicates that Jesus did not inform His disciples that the fourth commandment would be made void after His death. Since the first six texts say nothing about the sacredness of Sunday, we are left with two remaining verses:

Acts 20:7

Some people believe Acts 20:7 offers evidence to support Sunday worship. They use this text to prove the apostles worshiped on Sunday. But notice what the text says, **"On the first day of the week we came together to break bread. Paul spoke to the people and, because he intended to leave the next day, kept on talking until midnight."** (Acts 20:7) In Bible times, a day began at sunset and ended the following evening. Since Creation, the rotation of the Earth has produced this unchanging process. (See Genesis 1:5.) The Jews in Christ's time regarded a day from evening to evening, and they observed the Sabbath from Friday sundown to Saturday sundown. This practice remains intact among orthodox Jews today. (Compare Luke 23:50-56 with Leviticus 23:32.)

Therefore, the timing described in Acts 20:7 is as follows: Paul stayed with the believers at Troas for seven days. (Acts 20:6) On the evening of the first day of the week, at supper time, the believers met to eat supper with Paul and to say good-bye to their dear friend. Remember, the first day of the week in Paul's time began Sabbath evening at sundown, or what we now call Saturday evening and of course, Saturday night followed. After supper, Paul preached until midnight, or Saturday midnight. A few hours later on Sunday morning, the first day of the week, he left Troas for Assos. So, Paul met with believers for supper and preached until midnight, Saturday night. Does a farewell supper and a Saturday night meeting change or abrogate the fourth commandment of God? No. Even if Paul chose to hold a worship service on Wednesday night, would his behavior make God's law void? No. Only God can declare His law void.

Some Bible students claim that the term "breaking of bread" indicates Paul's visit was a communion or worship service. This is not true. In Luke 24:13-31 Jesus "broke bread" at supper time with His disciples after walking more than seven miles to Emmaus with them on the first day of the week. The breaking of bread, even to this day, remains a Middle Eastern custom since bread is often baked so firm that it has to be literally broken in order to be eaten. We know that Jesus "broke bread" on Thursday night with His disciples at Passover and the road to Emmaus experience happened Sunday evening just as Monday was beginning. Why would Jesus conduct a worship service at sundown in Emmaus, as the second day of the week was beginning? Even if it was a worship service, where is God's command to make void His fourth commandment? Certainly not in Acts 20:7.

Paul did not conduct a Sunday worship service in Troas because the day of worship had been changed. Actually, Paul held a farewell meeting on Saturday night – the first part of the first day of the week – after resting on the Sabbath. This story confuses a lot of people today, because we reckon a day from midnight to midnight. So, if Christians want to follow Paul's example as to "when" they should worship, they would need to worship on Saturday night (sundown to midnight). But still the question remains – where is the authority in this text for Sunday observance?

1 Corinthians 16:2

Some Christians argue that Paul insisted on taking an offering for the poor on the first day of the week. Notice: **"Now about the collection for God's people: Do what I told the Galatian churches to do. On the first day of every week, each one of you should set aside a sum of money in keeping with his income, saving it up, so that when I come no collections will have to be made. Then, when I arrive, I will give letters of introduction to the men you approve and send them with your gift to Jerusalem."** (1 Corinthians 16:1-3)

In Paul's day, money as a medium of exchange was not as common as it is today. Instead, trading was done through a barter system. For example, a person might trade a chicken or some other item for cloth or pottery. So, Paul instructed the church in Corinth to start early – begin the week with an attempt to exchange items for currency since it might take six days to do so. Paul wanted to carry money with him to help persecuted believers in Jerusalem. Paul did not want to travel with roosters, goats, pottery and other things of value, so he asked that they take care of this matter, **"first thing after the Sabbath."** (Compare with Nehemiah 13:15.) Again the question has to be raised, does Paul's instruction change or make void the fourth commandment of God? The answer is "No."

Thoughts on Romans 6

Many Christians, without offering any biblical support, claim that Sunday worship is God's will because Jesus arose from the dead on Sunday morning, the first day of the week. Yes, Jesus rose from the dead on Sunday and the resurrection is very important, but the Bible provides a celebration of the resurrection and it is not Sunday worship! It is baptism. Notice what Paul says, **"What shall we say, then? Shall we go on sinning so that grace may increase? By no means! We died to sin; how can we live in it any longer? Or don't you know that all of us who were baptized into Christ Jesus were baptized into his death? We were therefore buried with him through baptism into death in order that, just as Christ was raised from the dead through the glory of the Father, we too may live a new life."** (Romans 6:1-4) Paul makes a beautiful analogy of baptism by comparing the resurrection of Jesus from the dead with the experience of being resurrected from the deadness of sin through being born again! Baptism is a public statement that life in Christ has begun. Still we have to ask, does baptism change or abrogate the fourth commandment? Not at all. In fact, not one of the eight texts in the New Testament says that the holiness of the seventh day was transferred to Sunday! There is no text in the Bible indicating that Sunday is a sacred day! In fact, the fourth commandment says Sunday is a work day!

Herein lies a big part of the coming controversy over worship. Satan has duped the religions of the world on the subject of worship and when God's truth shines upon humanity, reinforced by overwhelming destruction everywhere, what will people do? The current mind set goes like this: If the Ten Commandments were nailed to the cross, and there is no command from God in the New Testament to worship God at any particular time, then God cannot be offended by man's diversity in worship. This mind set will be reversed when God's wrath spills over.

What Was Nailed to the Cross?

Many Christians argue that the Ten Commandments were nailed to the cross. Yet, this argument does not solve the problem. Whatever happens to the fourth commandment, happens to the other nine! If we do away with the fourth commandment that declares the seventh day to be a holy day, we must also do away with the commandment that says adultery is wrong. About 30 years after Jesus ascended, Paul wrote, **"What shall we say, then? Is the law sin? Certainly not! Indeed I would not have known what sin was except through the law. For I would not have known what coveting really was if *the law* had not said, 'Do not covet.' "** (Romans 7:7, italics mine) To what is Paul referring when he says "the law," if not the Ten Commandments?

So, what was nailed to the cross? When Jesus died, the Levitical system came to an end. The ceremonial system was terminated. Many Christians do not realize the ceremonies under the Levitical system were a shadow or illustration revealing the plan of salvation. The key word here is *shadow*. These shadow services pointed toward realities! (Hebrews 7 and 8) Paul writes, **"For in Christ all the fullness of the Deity lives in bodily form, and you have been given fullness in Christ, who is the head over every power and authority. . . . When you were dead in your sins and in the uncircumcision of your sinful nature, God made you alive with Christ. He forgave us all our sins, having canceled the written code, with its regulations, that was against us and that stood opposed to us; he took it away, nailing it to the cross. . . . Therefore do not let anyone judge you by what you eat or drink, or with regard to a religious festival, a New Moon celebration or a Sabbath day [feast]. *These are a shadow* of the things that were to come; the reality, however, is found in Christ. Do not let anyone who delights in false humility and the worship**

of angels disqualify you for the prize . . . ." (Colossians 2:9-18, insertion and italics mine)

If you look at these verses carefully, you can see that Paul is discussing things that were *shadows* of things to come. Of all the concepts taught in the Bible, the services in God's temple are among the most profound, intricate and beautiful. A proper understanding of these services ties all Bible themes together and they provide a backdrop against which all conclusions about God's will and ways can be tested and verified. This is a crucial point. God commanded Moses to set up a careful parallel or *shadow* of *the plan of salvation* so that human beings could study, test and validate their understanding of His marvelous ways by studying the shadow. God warned Moses to follow the pattern that God gave him. This makes sense because if the model was flawed, our study of Heaven's temple would also be flawed. Notice this verse: **"They** [the priests] **serve at a sanctuary that is a copy and *shadow* of what is in heaven. This is why Moses was warned when he was about to build the tabernacle: 'See to it that you make everything according to the pattern shown you on the mountain.'** " (Hebrews 8:5, insertion and italics mine)

New Moon observances and Sabbath day feasts were shadows required under the Levitical system. The "Sabbath day" that Paul is referring to is not the seventh day Sabbath of the fourth commandment. Rather, the term "Sabbath days" applies to feast days, such as the Passover, Pentecost or the Day of Atonement. (Leviticus 16:30-31) Certain feast days fell on different days of the week (like our birthday) because they occurred on the *same date* each year. These feast days were considered special Sabbaths of rest (or Sabbath days) that pointed forward to different aspects of the plan of salvation. For example, the Passover not only reminded the Jews of deliverance from Egypt, it also pointed forward to the time when the Passover Lamb – Jesus Christ – would die on the cross so the blood of God's firstborn Son could be applied to the doorposts of our hearts.

The Jews confused the Ten Commandment law of God with the laws of Moses much like Christians do today. The Jews did not understand the vibrant relationship between the covenant (written by God's finger) and the ceremonial laws (written by Moses' hand). One law was permanent, and the other was temporary. The greater law, the covenant or the Ten Commandments written by Jesus Himself, was kept inside the ark. (Hebrews 9:4) This is why the ark was called the ark of the "covenant." The lesser law of Moses, containing the *shadow* rules, was kept in a pocket on the outside of the ark. (See Deuteronomy 10:1,2; 31:26.) When Jesus died, the ceremonial rules, which were shadows of realities from their inception, ended. The relationship between the Ten Commandments and the laws written by Moses can be compared to the lesser/greater relationship that exists between state and federal laws in the United States. A state law cannot make a federal law void, but a federal law will eventually terminate a state law. This feature is necessary to preserve the union of the states.

Other Objections

Some Christians use Romans 14 to prove that it does not matter which day of the week we use to worship God. Notice the text: **"Accept him whose faith is weak, without passing judgment on disputable matters. One man's faith allows him to eat everything, but another man, whose faith is weak, eats only vegetables. The man who eats everything must not look down on him who does not, and the man who does not eat everything must not condemn the man who does, for God has accepted him. Who are you to judge someone else's servant? To his own master he stands or falls. And he will stand, for the Lord is able to make him stand. One man considers one day more sacred than another; another man considers every day alike. Each one should be fully convinced in his own mind. He who regards one day as special, does so to the Lord. He who eats meat, eats to the Lord, for** he gives thanks to God; and he who abstains, does so to the Lord and gives thanks to God. For none of us lives to himself alone and none of us dies to himself alone. If we live, we live to the Lord; and if we die, we die to the Lord. So, whether we live or die, we belong to the Lord. For this very reason, Christ died and returned to life so that he might be the Lord of both the dead and the living. You, then, why do you judge your brother? Or why do you look down on your brother? For we will all stand before God's judgment seat." (Romans 14:1-10)

These verses do not imply that we can worship God whenever we want. No, this text addresses a specific problem that early Roman Christians had to deal with; namely, the religious customs of newly converted Jews. In other words, if a new believer in Jesus felt he needed to continue to observe Passover, Paul did not condemn the new believer except to say that his faith was weak. Also, if the new believer could not consciously eat meat purchased in the marketplace for fear it had not been killed correctly or that it had been offered before idols, Paul's counsel was to leave him alone! (The Jews could not purchase nor eat meat unless it was killed according to Mosaic code. Leviticus 19:26) Today, many Christians use this text to support Sunday worship, although it says nothing about Sunday! I seriously doubt religious leaders will offer the freedom mentioned in these verses when they seek the exaltation of their country's day of worship through the enforcement of law during the Great Tribulation.

Sabbath Restated in New Testament

Some Christians claim that nine of the Ten Commandments are mentioned in the New Testament, but the fourth commandment is not restated. Therefore, because the fourth commandment was not mentioned in the New Testament, it *proves* the Sabbath commandment was voided when Jesus died on the cross. This statement is blatantly false because the fourth commandment is clearly affirmed in the New Testament! Paul wrote, **"There remains, then, a Sabbath-rest** for the people of God; for anyone who enters God's rest also rests from his own work, just as God did from his." (Hebrews 4:9,10) Believers in Christ will rest from their works "just as God did." *When* did God rest from His labors? Genesis 2:1-3 says He rested on the seventh day. Can the obligation of the seventh day Sabbath in the New Testament be any clearer? Paul faithfully observed the seventh day Sabbath during his lifetime. (See Acts 13:44; 16:13; 17:2; 18:4,11.) Even more, Jesus Himself, called attention to the fact that the seventh day Sabbath would remain sacred long after His ascension! (Matthew 24:20)

God's Law

The apostle Paul knew the Ten Commandments were intact after the cross. He said, **"For I would not have known what it was to covet if the law had not said, 'Do not covet.' "** (Romans 7:7) Likewise, James knew the Ten Commandments were intact after the cross. He wrote, **"If you really keep the royal law found in Scripture, 'Love your neighbor as yourself,' you are doing right! But if you show favoritism, you sin and are convicted by the law as lawbreakers. For whoever keeps the whole law and yet stumbles at just one point is guilty of breaking all of it. For he who said, 'Do not commit adultery,' also said, 'Do not murder.' If you do not commit adultery but do commit murder, you have become a lawbreaker."** (James 2:8-11) If the royal law includes "Do not commit adultery" and "Do not commit murder," the royal law has to include "Remember to keep the Sabbath holy." James highlights an important point about God's law we have to understand. James says that we have to obey *all* of the Ten Commandments. If we break one, we are guilty of breaking them all because the King's law is fulfilled through *total* submission to a God of love. Our love for God must be unlimited – with all our heart, mind and soul and also love for our neighbor should be equal to the love we have for ourselves. Jesus said, **"If you love me, you will obey what I command."** (John 14:15)

Chapter 7

A Dramatic Rescue by Jesus

World War III

The fifth trumpet marks the appearing of the devil and his angels. God permits the devil and his angels to occupy the nations of Earth and torment people who have not made a decision for God or the devil. For a five month period, God will allow the devil to inflict great suffering upon the remaining people who have not accepted salvation, but have defied the devil's authority. In this way, God continues to encourage them to repent and be saved. (For awhile, there will be two types of wicked people during the Great Tribulation: The "religious" wicked and the "nonreligious" wicked. The religious wicked are those who *believe* the devil is God and submit to his dominion. The nonreligious wicked are those who *refuse* to submit to the devil, God, or any authority.) When the five months have expired, God permits the devil to do something unbelievably horrible. Satan will be allowed to kill one-third of mankind. This great slaughter will remove most of the devil's adversaries, i.e., the nonreligious wicked and many of the saints. With most of his enemies dead (some saints will escape), the devil will have undisputed dominion over the Earth. When this occurs, the devil will then divide Earth into ten sectors and appoint ten "puppet" kings to take care of day to day business. By doing this, the devil will claim to be king of kings and lord of lords. Survivors will have no option; either submit to the commandments of the devil or suffer death. How ironic, those who submit to the commandments of Jesus may suffer temporary death, but they will live again!

God permits Satan to kill the nonreligious wicked at a very precise moment in time. Notice what John says, **"The sixth angel blew his trumpet . . . and the four angels (bound** at the great river Euphrates) who had been kept ready for this very hour and day and month and year were released to kill a third of mankind. The number of mounted troops was two hundred million. I heard their number . . . A third of mankind was killed by the three plagues of fire, smoke and sulfur that came out of their mouths. The rest of mankind that were not killed by these plagues still did not repent of the work of their hands . . . nor of their murders, their magic arts, their sexual immorality or their thefts." (Revelation 9:13-21)

What Satan cannot achieve through deceit, he accomplishes through force. Force is always the last resort of false religion. The sixth trumpet war will decimate all of the nations of the world. This is why I call this period of time World War III. Satan will send his angels throughout the Earth and they will slaughter hundreds of millions of people who stand in opposition to Satan's control of Earth. This great slaughter will accomplish two things. First, it will force everyone to take a side. Every living person will be forced to choose whom they will worship – the "lamb-like" beast on Earth claiming to be God, or the Lamb of God who will soon appear in clouds of glory. Second, when the devil gains control of Earth, he will be in a position to force everyone to receive his mark. **"He also *forced* everyone, small and great, rich and poor, free and slave, to receive a mark on his right hand or on his forehead."** (Revelation 13:16, italics mine)

Worship at Last

The Bible predicts the devil will lead a majority of the world to rebel against God's law. When the devil establishes his kingdom and implements the mark of the beast, he will require the world to worship on a day of the week that stands in direct opposition to the law of God. I am convinced the devil will declare a day of the week to be holy which opposes all religions of the world. In other words, a "new day" of worship will level the playing field for all religions of the world proving the devil shows no favoritism. Masquerading as God, the devil will be able to do anything he wants to do! No wonder Paul calls him a man of lawlessness. (2 Thessalonians 2) The devil will pronounce stringent laws requiring everyone to worship according to his desires. (Revelation 13:15-17) Of course, the devil's deepest desire is to have complete control and great adulation. He wants the same authority as God and he wants to be worshiped as God. The devil is very bold. He even dared to tempt Jesus to worship him. (Matthew 4:9,10) Satan may be incredibly beautiful in appearance, but he will be grossly vile in character. He is sin personified. The devil is self seeking and self centered in the extreme. The devil wants power, fame, popularity, respect, wealth, glory and honor. He will allow nothing to stand in his way of gaining these. In fact, he wants everything that rightfully belongs to God! What an example of sin's decadence. Remember, God created Lucifer as a perfect being. However, sin corrupted Lucifer's heart and he assumed prerogatives belonging only to God. Ultimately, Lucifer will claim before the world that he is God. He will receive the worship that God alone deserves and he will gloat in his deception. Paul says, **"He [Satan] opposes and exalts himself over everything that is called God or is worshiped, and even sets himself up in God's temple, proclaiming himself to be God."** (2 Thessalonians 2:4)

The Offer of Salvation Ends

When the slaughter of World War III ends, everyone will have made a decision about worship. For the sake of survival, millions will submit to the commandments of the Antichrist even though they know the mark of the beast is a curse. Remember, worship is defined as submitting to a requirement commanded by God. It is hard to believe that people would submit to the mark of the beast rather than put faith in God, but this will be the case. Consider the wisdom behind this coming test of faith: If our worship of God is not based on faith and love for Jesus, it will be impossible to refuse the mark of the beast. The saints will lose every form of earthly support. It is easy to see how many people who claim to be Christians will give up their religious beliefs because their faith is not grounded in God.

They will voluntarily receive the mark of the beast and justify their actions because it is the only way to survive. I have heard people say many times that they cannot keep Sabbath because they cannot give up their job! If a person loves his life more than God – he does not love God most – he loves self! Jesus said, **"Anyone who loves his father or mother more than me is not worthy of me; anyone who loves his son or daughter more than me is not worthy of me; and anyone who does not take his cross and follow me is not worthy of me. Whoever finds his life will lose it, and whoever loses his life for my sake will find it."** (Matthew 10:37-39)

Everyone who chooses to receive the mark of the beast will be a coward and considered an enemy of God. (Revelation 21:8) When the sixth trumpet war draws to a close, everyone will have made their decision and nothing more can be done to save a single human being. Consequently, the door to salvation closes in Heaven and Jesus concludes His intercession on behalf of the people of Earth with this decree: **"Let him who does wrong continue to do wrong; let him who is vile continue to be vile; let him who does right continue to do right; and let him who is holy continue to be holy."** (Revelation 22:11) Then, **"The seventh angel sounded his trumpet, and there were loud voices in heaven, which said: 'The kingdom of the world has become the kingdom of our Lord and of his Christ, and he will reign for ever and ever.' . . . Then God's temple in heaven was opened, and within his temple was seen the ark of his covenant. And there came flashes of lightning, rumblings, peals of thunder, an earthquake and a great hailstorm."** (Revelation 11:15,19)

The seventh trumpet marks the end of God's redemptive judgments. (Do not confuse the seventh trumpet with the trumpet call that sounds from the sky at the Second Coming. 1 Corinthians 15:52) The seventh trumpet also marks the beginning of God's destructive judgments (the seven bowls). Notice, the *same* phenomena that marks the beginning of the seven trumpets also marks the end of the seven trumpets.

(Revelation 8:5) However, the phenomena at the end of the seven trumpets will be greater in intensity and more destructive than at the beginning of the Great Tribulation. In addition to these physical phenomena, God will do something at the close of salvation that is amazing. He will enable everyone on Earth to see the ark of "His covenant" in Heaven's temple! God shows the Ark of the Covenant to the human race because He wants everyone to see the lawful basis for His wrath. He is about to destroy every wicked person with one or more of the seven last plagues. God wants the wicked to *see* that His wrath is legally justified. This is a marvelous thing about God. In God's realm, faith *always* precedes evidence. Paul wrote, **"When perfection comes, the imperfect disappears."** (1 Corinthians 13:10) In other words, whenever God commands something that requires faith, He eventually displaces that faith with the evidence or reason faith was necessary. Said another way, faith always makes sense when viewed in reverse. Jesus said, **"I tell you the truth, until Heaven and Earth disappear, not the smallest letter, not the least stroke of a pen, will by any means disappear from the Law until everything is accomplished."** (Matthew 5:18) This is why salvation comes only through faith! God says, "You just have to trust Me until I can show you the reasons."

Only the Faith-full Will Survive

Standing firm for truth and worshiping God as He commands regardless of the cost will be the all encompassing test for the human race. Hundreds of millions of people will die for their faith. Relatively speaking, only a few saints will survive to see Jesus appear in clouds of glory. John is very clear – the devil's forces will kill a large number of God's people. Mercifully, when the seventh trumpet sounds, God ends the martyrdom of the saints. (Daniel 12:1) Can we, like Job, say, **"Though He slay me, yet will I hope in Him"**? (Job 13:15) A real testing time is just before us. The coming test will reveal our true condition. Will we stand firm even though everyone else may join the ranks of the enemy? I pray God will give us the faith, resolve and strength to stand firm. Isaiah said it well when he spoke to King Ahaz, **"If you do not stand firm in your faith, you will not stand at all."** (Isaiah 7:9)

The Seven Bowls

The seven bowls will begin shortly after God reveals the Ark of the Covenant in the sky and last for about 75 days. The seven bowls will be progressively destructive and end with Jesus appearing in clouds of glory. Jesus will kill the wicked by a command that comes out of His mouth. Only the saints who remain will survive that awesome day. The seven last plagues will be a horrible *payback* for the wicked. The seven *last* plagues contain God's wrath without mercy – God's wrath full strength. God will repay the wicked at the same level of cruelty they demonstrated towards God's people during the Great Tribulation. Compare the seven trumpets with the seven bowls:

Trumpets	Bowls
1. Fiery hail	1. Terrible sores
2. Asteroid impact (Sea)	2. Sea turns to blood
3. Asteroid impact (Continent)	3. Springs of waters turn to blood
4. Darkness (Volcanos)	4. Sun scorches people with fire
5. Devil appears	5. Satan's kingdom plunged into darkness
6. Devil conquers world	6. Armageddon
7. Close of mercy	7. Second coming / Great fiery hail stones

Remember, these seven plagues do not affect God's people. **"A thousand may fall at your side, ten thousand at your right hand, but it will not come near you. You will only observe with your eyes the punishment of the wicked."** (Psalm 91:7,8)

Three points need to be made:

1. Some of the seven bowls are somewhat similar to the destruction caused by the seven trumpets. For example, a third of the seas turn to blood during the second trumpet, but all of the seas turn to blood during the second bowl. Perhaps God designed the trumpets as harbingers of things to come. In other words, even though the trumpets are sounded with mercy, God uses the trumpets to warn the human race with some physical evidence of what He intends to do during the seven bowls, a time when there is no mercy! Remember, God spares two-thirds of Earth during the time period of the seven trumpets, but He annihilates the entire world with burning sulfur at the end of the seven bowls.

2. Notice this turn of events. The *fifth* trumpet marks the physical appearing of Satan claiming to be God and the *fifth* bowl marks the exposure of the devil for who he really is. When Jesus pours out the fifth plague upon the throne of the devil, the world will see that this creature, who claims to be God, is not really God – for God would not destroy His own throne! (See Revelation 16:10,11.) The light of truth will shine brightly, and the deception of sin will be removed. The religious and political leaders of the world will realize they have been worshiping the ancient enemy of God. This realization starts a domino-like collapse of Babylon. John says, **"The beast** [Babylon] **and the ten horns you saw will hate the prostitute** [the image or the one world church/state]. **They will bring her to ruin and leave her naked; they will eat her flesh and burn her with fire."** (Revelation 17:16)

3. In a final attempt to control a collapsing kingdom, Satan will rally the world one last time and send powerful demons to encourage the ten kings he chose to rule over Earth. These demons will lead the kings of the Earth to do two things. First, they will agree that a universal death decree is needed to destroy the saints. Second, they will unite to wage war on Jesus when He appears in the clouds. Notice what John says of these demons, **"They are the spirits of demons performing**

miraculous signs, and they go out to the kings of the whole world, to gather them for the battle on the great day of God Almighty. . . . Then they gathered the kings together to the place that in Hebrew is called Armageddon." (Revelation 16:14, 16)

Armageddon – The Final Battle

World War III occurs during the sixth trumpet. The battle of Armageddon occurs during the sixth bowl. (Remember, there are similarities between the trumpets and bowls.) A large amount of misinformation has been shared about Armageddon. The word, Armageddon, comes from two Greek words, *"har megiddon"* and they are transliterated in English as one word: Armageddon. The two words mean "the mountain of God," or "the exalted place of God." There is no mountain in the Middle East called Meggido; however, there is a small plain called Meggido that is not far from Jerusalem. (Joshua 17:11) Long ago, King Josiah's foolish actions led to his death on the Plain of Meggido. He engaged Pharaoh Neco in a battle that should not have been fought. (2 Chronicles 35) The plain of Megiddo is not very large, but many scholars are convinced this is where Earth's last battle will be fought.

The battle of Armageddon parallels the contest between Elijah and the 450 prophets of Baal on Mount Carmel. (1 Kings 18) A showdown is coming between the Lamb of God and the lamb-like beast, who is the devil. This great showdown will occur "on the mountain of God," hence the two words, *"har megiddon."* The world's leaders will see, just as the leaders of Israel did in Elijah's day, which God is Almighty God.

Here is the scenario: After God unmasks the devil in the fifth bowl, the devil's empire will begin to disintegrate. The religious and political leaders of Babylon will recognize they have been duped into worshiping the devil. Then, *the cloud* will appear in the sky – the sign of Christ's return. **"At that time the *sign* of the Son of Man will appear in the sky, and all the nations of the earth will mourn."** (Matthew 24:30, italics mine) When the kings of Earth see the sign in the sky, they will tremble. The devil preys on their anxiety and will invite them to join him in a two pronged attack. He insists they can kill the remaining saints at an appointed hour and then attack Jesus as He draws near to Earth. (Once again, truth is stranger than fiction.) To convince the kings of Earth this is their last chance to save themselves from destruction, the devil sends three powerful demons to help persuade them. **"They are spirits of demons performing miraculous signs, and they go out to the kings of the whole world, to gather them for the battle on the great day of God Almighty."** (Revelation 16:14) When the kings of Earth see the miracle working powers of these three demons, the leaders will be compelled to trust their power and will agree to join forces with the devil. (What choice do they really have?) They will make plans to destroy the people Jesus is coming to save and ultimately to kill Jesus Himself. If you think that it is far fetched that men would try to kill God, remember the cross. If you think it is far fetched that angels would war against an omnipotent God, consider Lucifer's expulsion from Heaven. When sin is allowed to reach its vilest maturity, it will seek to destroy God. Sinners would attempt to kill God (if they could) if pushed to worship Him! This is why God has to completely eliminate sin from His universe. Sin is a cancer from which there is no recovery – except through the "born again" experience.

The battle of Armageddon occurs at the place of God's choosing – the mountain of God. It will be the last battle of Earth's final generation. The wicked will see this as their only chance to destroy God. John describes the scene this way: **"The seventh angel poured out his bowl into the air, and out of the temple came a loud voice from the throne saying, 'It is done.' Then there came flashes of lightning, rumblings, peals of thunder and a severe earthquake. No earthquake like it has ever occurred since man has been on earth, so tremendous was the quake. The great city split into three parts, and the cities of the nations collapsed. God remembered Babylon the Great and gave her the cup filled with the wine of the fury of his wrath. Every island fled away and the mountains could not be found.**

From the sky huge hailstones of about a hundred pounds each fell upon men. And they cursed God on account of the plague of hail, because the plague was so terrible." (Revelation 16:17-21)

John also describes the behavior of the wicked: "**They called ... to the mountains and the rocks, 'Fall on us and hide us from the face of him who sits on the throne and from the wrath of the Lamb! For the great day of their wrath has come, and who can stand?'**" (Revelation 6:16,17) Paul says Jesus will destroy the physical body of the devil with a single command: "**And then the lawless one** [the man of sin] **will be revealed, whom the Lord Jesus will overthrow with the breath of his mouth and destroy by the splendor of his coming.**" (2 Thessalonians 2:8, insertion mine) What a sight this will be – fire falling from Heaven and consuming the physical body of the devil and his angels! Zephaniah says, "**Neither their silver nor their gold will be able to save them on the day of the Lord's wrath. In the fire of his jealousy the whole world will be consumed, for he will make a sudden end of all who live in the Earth.**" (Zephaniah 1:18) What a dramatic rescue! What an amazing God! What a Savior is Jesus our Lord! What a Friend the saints have in Jesus. Is it possible that some of Satan's forces perish on the plain of Meggido? Perhaps, since one of Satan's thrones may be located in Jerusalem (Daniel 11:45), but remember, Satan will have ten kings fighting against Jesus. These kings will represent *all* of the nations of the world.

Review

There are several powerful stories in the book of Revelation that have not been addressed in this small book. This book has briefly addressed the seven trumpets and the seven bowls. There is much more. Therefore, I hope you will consider this book to be a first step toward a better understanding of Revelation.

Because the book of Revelation is about the revelation of Jesus Christ, I am compelled to close with a review of the gospel of Jesus Christ and an invitation to worship Him. Reviewing the gospel is necessary because it confronts us with an all or nothing proposition. Before the seventh trumpet sounds, all of the inhabitants of Earth will either accept or reject the gospel of Jesus. Some people avoid difficult decisions by putting them off into the recesses of consciousness. They say, "I will think about this tomorrow." However, postponement is really a decision, too. Suppose you are a young man who asked your sweetheart to marry you. Any answer other than "yes" is actually a "no," isn't it? The danger with postponement is that it hides our rejection until we are trapped by our own inaction. In the case of the gospel, we must listen and respond to the Holy Spirit promptly or the Spirit may turn away from us. We must be "born again" today and this transformation cannot be accomplished on our own. Only through the ministry of the Holy Spirit can we overcome the rebellion of our carnal nature. Therefore, it is important to remember that there is a limit to the Holy Spirit's promptings. He will not wrestle with rebellion forever. (Hebrews 3:7-15; 10:26)

If the Holy Spirit has impressed you that this message is important, you need to restudy it carefully for two reasons. First, your understanding will increase 100% the second time you read this book. Details will become clearer and more meaningful. Second, now that you understand the general picture of Revelation, you need to find an interested friend and discuss this message. You may want to obtain some of the study materials listed in the back of this book. The better we understand God's Word, the stronger our faith will be. Jesus is coming soon. Until the seventh trumpet sounds, the door of mercy is open. Walk through it! **"The Spirit and the bride say, 'Come!' And let him who hears say, 'Come!' Whoever is thirsty, let him come; and whoever wishes, let him take the free gift of the water of life."** (Revelation 22:17)

The Proclamation of the Gospel

The gospel of Jesus Christ will reach every person before Jesus comes. John said, **"Then I saw another angel flying in midair, and he had the eternal gospel to proclaim to**

those who live on the Earth to every nation, tribe, language and people." (Revelation 14:6) Jesus said, **"And this gospel of the kingdom will be preached in the whole world as a testimony to all nations, and then the end will come."** (Matthew 24:14) What gospel will be preached into all the world before the end of salvation comes? In three sentences, the eternal gospel of Jesus Christ is this: *All people have sinned and come short of the glory of God (everyone has violated God's Ten Commandments at some point in time); therefore, God's law condemns us to death (the wages of sin is death). The good news is that Jesus took our place on the cross and paid the price for our sins. If we obediently submit to God's commandments and put our faith in Jesus for salvation, we will be saved.* Look at salvation from God's perspective. Many people honestly live up to all they know to be right and Jesus understands this. In His great mercy, He accepts everyone who is sincere in heart even though they may not know or understand the great truths of the gospel. Jesus does not hold a person responsible for truth he does not know or cannot know. On the contrary, James tells us that sin is held against us when we know better and then refuse to do it! **"Anyone, then, who knows the good he ought to do and doesn't do it, sins."** (James 4:17) The Lord loves the people of Earth with a love beyond human understanding. He died for every one of us. People who live up to all they know to be right glorify God and He is pleased with them. Peter says, **"For the eyes of the Lord are on the righteous and his ears are attentive to their prayer, but the face of the Lord is against those who do evil."** (1 Peter 3:12) Because the devil is extremely intelligent, Satan has cleverly obscured God's truth from most of the world, but Jesus will soon remove the veil of ignorance that covers the gospel. People who are sincere in heart will rejoice to learn more, and they will embrace the gospel as it reveals more about the will of our Creator and Savior. Thus, a remnant from all religious systems will be gathered into one body under the leadership of King Jesus. Jesus said, **"I have other sheep that are not of this sheep pen. I must bring them also. They too will listen to my voice, and there shall be one flock and one shepherd."** (John 10:16)

So, the net effect of the gospel in the last days will be to save and unify all people who hear and respond to the voice of Jesus. Jesus will accomplish this ingathering of His sheep during the 1,260 day time period allotted for the seven trumpets by separating His sheep from the goats over the issue of worship. (Matthew 25:31-46) People will either receive the gospel and through faith, obey the commandments of Jesus or they will reject the gospel and eventually choose the mark of the beast. The controversy over worship will remove all middle ground. A rapid sequence of events, coupled with rigorous laws requiring that people disobey the law of God will push everyone into a decision.

What Must I Do to be Saved?

As we might expect, Satan has a counterfeit gospel. The devil has led many people to believe that salvation comes either through perfect obedience to God (as in human performance) or by intellectual assent to what is true. Satan's deceptions are very subtle. He has led many evil people to think they are righteous when they are far from it! Nevertheless, the Bible is clear, the righteousness necessary for salvation is not found on Earth! **"For in the gospel a righteousness from God is revealed, a righteousness that is by faith from first to last, just as it is written: 'The righteous will live by faith'. . . . This righteousness from God comes through faith in Jesus Christ to all who believe. There is no difference, for all have sinned and fall short of the glory of God, and are justified freely by his grace through the redemption that came by Christ Jesus."** (Romans 1:17; 3:22-24) Satan ever leads people astray and away from God. The Pharisees thought they were righteous in God's sight even though they were not a part of the kingdom of God. Jesus said, **". . . on the outside you [Pharisees] appear to people as righteous but on the inside you are full of hypocrisy and wickedness . . . For I tell you that unless your righteousness surpasses that of the Pharisees and the teachers of the law, you will certainly not enter the kingdom of**

Heaven." (Matthew 23:28; 5:20, insertion mine) The Pharisees were known for their love of self righteousness. They could not see their own sins but they could see sin in a sinless Jesus. (John 9:16) Isn't it ironic that religion can lead a person to condemn God and justify self! This is ever the human dilemma. Religion tends to blind people to their true condition in God's sight. Given enough time, all religions eventually distort the truth about God – history proves this is the way of mankind.

Yes, God is pleased when we love to do what is right, but contrary to what the Pharisees believed, right doing does not save us! So, how are we saved? We are saved through faith in Jesus. True worship stems from a Spirit given desire to please God. (John 4:23,24) True worship includes doing all that we understand God wants us to do, not to be saved, but to please God! *The worship of Jesus Christ is the way to salvation and this is why God's final test of mankind centers on worship!* (John 10:7; 14:6) People who worship God with all their heart, mind and soul are willing to go, to be and to do all that God requires – no holds barred. *Jesus has designed the events of the Great Tribulation so that only those who love and trust Him completely will be able to worship Him on His holy day.* "The just will live by faith." True worshipers worship God in Spirit and in Truth. All who worship God are given the righteousness necessary for salvation and the amazing aspect of this is that salvation is free! (Ephesians 2:8,9)

Jesus said, "**. . . every good tree bears good fruit, a good tree cannot bear bad fruit, but a bad tree bears bad fruit, and a bad tree cannot bear good fruit.**" (Matthew 7:17,18) A counterfeit gospel causes sinners to think they are righteous. The carnal heart will say one thing in public, but do evil in secret. Jesus said, "**Everyone who does evil hates the light, and will not come into the light for fear that his deeds will be exposed. But whoever lives by the truth comes into the light, so that it may be seen plainly that what he has done has been done through God.**" (John 3:20,21) So, we must test ourselves from time to time to see if we are in Christ! Paul wrote, **"Examine yourselves to see whether you are in the faith; test yourselves. Do you not realize that Christ Jesus is in you – unless, of course, you fail the test?"** (2 Corinthians 13:5)

Trust and Obey

James Sammis and Daniel Towner wrote the old gospel hymn, "Trust and Obey." The words are printed below because they summarize the essence of the gospel of Jesus very well:

> "When we walk with the Lord
> In the light of His Word,
> What a glory He sheds on our way!
> While we do His good will,
> He abides with us still,
> And with all who will trust and obey.
> Trust and obey,
> For there's no other way
> To be happy in Jesus,
> But to trust and obey."

It never ceases to amaze me that so many Christians scoff at the suggestion that the Lord will return soon. They see no reason for this warning message. They say, "All things continue as usual – why all the fuss?" Unfortunately, these people have become content in their spiritual poverty. They have put blinders on and inserted earplugs because they are comfortable and do not want to hear about God's plan. Many Christians follow after religious programming, i.e., the entertainment gospel presented by talented singers and gifted speakers with clever ideas. They do not want to hear about the cross they will bear during the time of God's wrath. Before we can wear a crown, we have to carry the cross. Millions of people believe in a pretribulation rapture. Satan has convinced many Christians they are safe from the scenes described in Revelation. This terrible deception is widely accepted because it is so easy to swallow. It is time for Christians to wake up and understand that Revelation will be fulfilled soon!

People who truly understand Revelation's story are not focused on gloom or doom. This may seem strange, but it is true. Instead, they are focused on the greatest and most awesome event in Earth's history: The revelation of the gospel of Jesus Christ during the Great Tribulation and His physical appearing at the Second Coming. We need to know that a testing time, a purifying time is coming, and it precedes the Second Coming. We need to know about the rise of Babylon and the appearing of Satan claiming to be God. We need to know about World War III and Armageddon. And yes, we need to fill our hearts and minds with God's Word because our faith in God will be fully tested in days to come. We have every reason to be positive about our relationship with Jesus for it is this relationship that fills our hearts with peace and joy. **"For everyone born of God overcomes the world. This is the victory that has overcome the world, even our faith. Who is it that overcomes the world? Only he who believes that Jesus is the Son of God."** (1 John 5:4,5) Believers in Christ have a wonderful opportunity to become overcomers for Christ. We carry God's promises within our hearts and listen to His voice because we "have ears to hear what the Spirit is saying to us." Believers walk by faith, not by sight.

I am often asked how a person should reconcile the nearness of these events with everyday decisions in life. For example, what does a person do about plans for college, marriage, building or buying a new home, the expansion of a business, retirement savings, career requirements, etc.? I have found one response for all of these questions: Seek the Lord for wisdom *about your own personal situation.* He has promised to direct us. If we patiently seek answers from Him, God will show us what He wants. (Proverbs 3:5-6) So, learn to live by faith now. Worship the Creator! Keep God's Sabbath holy. Doing so will provide a whole day each week to study God's Word. Put your confidence in God and watch what He will do through you and for you. The ultimate test of having a relationship with Jesus is being able to hear His voice. Jesus said, **"My sheep listen to my voice; I know them, and they follow me."** (John 10:27)

Appendix
Comments by the Author

I believe most of the prophetic interpretations we hear on radio or see on television today are wrong. I do not make this statement carelessly or arrogantly for I accept the possibility that I too, could be wrong. In fact, I have been wrong in times past in my understanding of God's Word and have published corrections indicating my errors. Of course, this admission bothers some people who think that religious views should be flawless and inerrant. This is nonsense. Who is flawless and inerrant on Earth? The only person on Earth to claim infallibility is the pope and according to the Bible, such a claim is false. *God alone is infinite and true* and everyone else is finite, including prophets and angels. (Do not forget, one-third of the angels were cast out of Heaven, so angels are not infallible either.) Knowledge ever advances and this is also true of our knowledge of God. If Henry Ford had known how to manufacture Lincoln Town Cars, would he have wasted his time manufacturing Model T's? Of course not! I have found a consistent process at work during my 30 years of Bible study. In order for my understanding of God's Word to grow, I have no other option than to let go of wrong ideas so that I can embrace more of God's truth. The process of letting go of errors in order to gain more truth makes it impossible for me to belong to a religious denomination, because denominations have fixed creeds. Every denomination has certain nonnegotiable positions and these fixed positions prevent them from moving forward. The good news, though, is that salvation is not dependent on belonging to some denomination! Jesus Christ will save anyone who is willing to worship Him.

My studies have led me to conclude that the extremely popular *"Left Behind"* series is a gross distortion of what the Bible teaches about the Great Tribulation. Do not misunderstand.

People are free to believe anything they choose to believe about the future and that freedom must not be restricted. However, what a person chooses to believe or not believe has no bearing on coming events (and this includes my conclusions as well). Almost everyone in Noah's day refused to believe a flood was coming. What effect did their denial have on the promised event? Zero. Unfortunately, millions of people have been led to anticipate things that will never happen and when the predicted events of Revelation occur, everyone's faith in God will be severely jolted. After the first four judgments take place and overwhelming destruction is everywhere, millions of people will be tempted to abandon their faith in God because they were unprepared. I am troubled that religious leaders are not informing and spiritually preparing their followers for the trying circumstances ahead! I believe many religious leaders are sincere, godly people, but are they searching for truth beyond denominational limits with due diligence? Bible truth is always unfolding, therefore Bible truth is always "outside the box." If you follow wherever the Bible leads, you will eventually find yourself "outside the box" in no time! The Bible clearly says a testing time is coming upon the Earth. (Revelation 3:10) Every person, pastor and layman alike, should be concerned about this predicted event!

The Ultimate Test

Of course, no prophetic expositor can prove his or her predictions about the future. It is impossible to prove the accuracy of a conclusion before it happens. However, there are two ways to *test* a prediction for accuracy. The most direct method is to record the prediction *before* the event comes to pass. Then, when the predicted event occurs, ordinary people can judge the accuracy of the prediction. This simple procedure allows an impartial jury of observers to decide which predictions and interpretations are accurate by simply noting the presence or absence of events which have been predicted.

The other way to test predictions about the future is to use a *valid* set of methods (rules or hermeneutics) that are "self evident" within the Bible. The mention of "methods" might be a new thought for some readers. *Methods of interpretation* has become a catchall phrase that has a lot of significance in the study of Bible prophecy. Actually, the phrase "methods of interpretation" describes a set of ideas in a person's head *before* he or she starts to study and interpret prophecy – ideas like religious views, spiritual presuppositions, scholastic assumptions and concepts about the role and authority of the Bible, prophets and church traditions. For example, a person from a particular religious persuasion might approach the study of Bible prophecy with a number of preconceived ideas, beliefs and traditions in his or her mind. His or her prophetic conclusions would naturally reflect these methods of interpretation. This is true for everyone from every walk of life. The point is that no one approaches the study of prophecy without some kind of intellectual or spiritual baggage in his or her head. This baggage is loosely defined as his or her "methods of interpretation." So, how does one eliminate baggage that is faulty? How does a person arrive at the intended meaning of Bible prophecy? This is a very tough question and I have spent many years trying to resolve it and here is what I have concluded:

The book of Daniel was written about 26 centuries ago, but unlike the other 65 books in the Bible, some of the prophecies in the book of Daniel were sealed up "until the time of the end." The angel, Gabriel, said to Daniel, "**. . . Go your way, Daniel, because the words are closed up and sealed until the time of the end.**" (Daniel 12:9) What does "closed up and sealed until the time of the end" mean? It means that certain information in the book of Daniel remains "top secret" until the time of the end arrives. My study of Bible prophecy has brought me to the conclusion that we are living chronologically "at the time of the end." If this conclusion is true, the time has come for the secrets of Daniel to be unveiled. (For a comprehensive study on the book of Daniel and other subjects, the reader is encouraged to examine materials offered on our web site *www.wake-up.org* or described at the end of this book.)

Rosetta Stone

The secret information coded into Daniel 2,600 years ago turns out to be something like the "Rosetta Stone." The Rosetta Stone was accidently unearthed in 1799 near Rosetta, Egypt, by French soldiers. The marvelous thing about this buried rock is that it bears a message that was written during the second century B.C. in both forms of Egyptian script, demotic and hieroglyphics. When archeologists discovered this ancient rock, they were able to solve a very perplexing mystery. Prior to 1799, archeologists had unearthed many clay tablets containing Egyptian hieroglyphics, but the tablets could not be deciphered because no one could read hieroglyphics. When the Rosetta Stone was discovered and translated, the demotic inscriptions on the Rosetta Stone enabled Thomas Young (1773-1829) and J.F. Champollion (1790-1832) to decipher the hieroglyphics of the ancient Egyptians for the first time. In a similar way, I believe God embedded four secrets in the book of Daniel a long time ago. These secrets have remained buried within the text of Daniel for almost 26 centuries. Now that we have come to the time of the end, it is time for the secrets of Daniel to be "unearthed." By God's grace alone, I believe my studies have led me to stumble into the secrets that were sealed up in the book of Daniel. (The passage of time, of course, will prove or disprove the validity of this claim.) If true, the discovery of these four secrets ruins two thousand years of prophetic exposition since, *All prophetic conclusions based on the book of Daniel have to be faulty until the time of the end when the book of Daniel is unsealed!* In other words, no one can know the truth about Daniel's prophecies until all of the necessary information is unsealed. Said another way, the book of Daniel was sealed up until the time of the end; therefore, only those people who live at the time of the end can know *the truth* about Daniel's prophecies.

Three Levels of Information

As a person might expect, God buried His secrets deeply in the book of Daniel. However, when God wants to bring understanding to the forefront, He enables ordinary men and women to discover what He has hidden. Through the ages we find this process at work: On or about the time of fulfillment, elements of prophecy are understood. For example, when it came time to understand the timing of Christ's birth, the wise men from the East figured it out. (Matthew 2:2) The apostle Paul also noticed this phenomenon. Consider his words: **"Surely you have heard about the administration of God's grace that was given to me for you, that is, the mystery made known to me by revelation, as I have already written briefly. In reading this, then, you will be able to understand my insight into the mystery of Christ, which was not made known to men in other generations as it has now been revealed by the Spirit to God's holy apostles and prophets. This mystery is that through the gospel the Gentiles are heirs together with Israel, members together of one body, and sharers together in the promise in Christ Jesus."** (Ephesians 3:2-6)

What did God hide in the book of Daniel? The answer to this question requires a little background explanation. The book of Daniel has three levels of understanding which are:

1. Dramatic stories of faith
2. Visions revealing God's plans
3. Apocalyptic architecture

The first level (or easiest) level of information in Daniel contains dramatic stories of faith in God. These stories of faith and loyalty to God were recorded to benefit all generations, but the generation that will benefit most from these displays of courage will be Earth's final generation. For example, the fiery trials found in the first chapters of Daniel are miniature parallels of coming events. In Daniel 3, we read about Shadrach, Meshach and Abednego facing a mandatory requirement to worship a golden *image set up by the king of Babylon.* In Revelation 13:15 we read about the inhabitants of the world facing a mandatory requirement to worship an *image set up by the king of modern Babylon.* These dramatic stories of faith were recorded in Daniel to benefit all generations, but especially for the final generation!

The second level (or more difficult level) of information concerns the content and meaning of the visions in the book of Daniel. The visions God gave to King Nebuchadnezzar and Daniel faithfully predict the passage of time and the fulfillment of all that God predestined to occur. Even more, the visions reveal what God planned to do before He told Nebuchadnezzar or Daniel of His plans. Because students of prophecy have understood (more or less) the meaning of Daniel's visions for hundreds of years, we cannot say the meaning of Daniel's visions were sealed until "the time of the end." However, one element within the book of Daniel was sealed up and uniquely applies to those people who *live at the end* of the world. What is it?

The Book Unsealed

The third level (and deepest level) of information found in Daniel is *the architecture of apocalyptic prophecy.* This may sound strange at first, but the prophecies in Daniel conform to a structure or pattern that controls the meaning of the visions given in Daniel. The exciting point about this structure is that the same structure also exists in Revelation! In other words, when you understand the architecture of Daniel, you also understand the architecture of Revelation. The architecture of apocalyptic prophecy produces four rules (methods of interpretation) that govern the interpretation of this type of prophecy. These four rules are like combinations to a safe. When the four rules are applied to the interpretation of the prophecies of Daniel, as well as Revelation, a marvelous result occurs. The prophecies can be understood *just as they read*! This is not a casual matter. Consider that certain elements in Daniel (and Revelation) remained a mystery for 2,600 years until one day, the words make sense just as they read! What makes the sudden difference? It is the understanding of how the architecture is constructed.

When the four rules found in Daniel are applied, a comprehensive story unfolds that is completely harmonious with everything the Bible has to say about the ways of God. Furthermore, all of the details God gave in the prophecies of Daniel and Revelation are in perfect harmony and synchrony with each other. The four rules force all of the prophecies in Daniel and Revelation to form a matrix of events that are chronological in nature. To visualize this matrix, think of the prophecies in Daniel and Revelation as 18 pieces of plywood of varying lengths that are stacked on top of each other. The longer pieces are at the bottom of the stack and the shorter pieces are cut to precise lengths so that they neatly fit within the dimensions of the longer ones. The nails that hold the 18 pieces of plywood together are the events that unite the 18 prophecies in Daniel and Revelation into one grand story. Often, two or more prophecies describe the same event. Because of this, precise alignment of the prophecies is not only possible, but essential to understanding the big picture.

The Value and Importance of Rules

Daniel's prophecies (and the elements within them) behave in a predictable way *every time*. This consistency allows us to understand certain things about the operation and meaning of apocalyptic prophecy that would be otherwise unknown. For example, we can say that all of Daniel's prophecies have a beginning point and an ending point in time, and the events in each prophecy occur in the order in which they are given. This concept may sound simple, but it has profound ramifications. Look at the down side of this rule: If the events within each prophecy are not fulfilled in the order given, then who or what has the authority to tell us the order of events that have not happened? In other words, if the Bible cannot be understood on the basis of what it says, then who has the truth on this matter? This is the ultimate question: Does the Bible speak for itself or must it have an interpreter? After many years of study, my mind is settled regarding this issue. I believe the Bible speaks for itself and the Bible is its final interpreter. The constant and predictable architecture within Daniel's prophecies is the basis for rule one. In my words the rule says, *"Each apocalyptic prophecy has a beginning point and an ending point in time and the events within each prophecy must occur in the order they are given."* Keep in mind that I am not fabricating this rule of interpretation. Rather, I am merely expressing in my own words a consistent behavior that I have found in the architecture of Daniel.

Everyone Follows Rules

Knowingly or unknowingly, each student of prophecy implements "a method of interpretation" to support his or her prophetic conclusions. The problem, of course, is that invalid rules cannot produce valid results. For example, some people believe this rule to be valid: "A day in Bible prophecy *always* equals a year." Advocates of this rule reason that if the seventy weeks of Daniel 9 represent 490 years (and they do), then all time periods in Daniel and Revelation have to be interpreted according to this rule. (A rule cannot have an exception, for if it does, it becomes impossible to determine when the rule should or should not be applied.) If the day/year rule is *always* true as some say, then the 1,000 years mentioned in Revelation 20 would be 365,242 years in length because there are 365.242 days per year. For many reasons, the day/year rule stated above is not valid, but this illustration does demonstrate how rules force people into making conclusions about prophecy. If all of the 18 prophetic time periods in Daniel and Revelation have to be interpreted according to the day/year rule, then timing issues will interfere with otherwise plain statements. If the rules are flawed or inadequate, prophetic expositors have to resort to some kind of nonsensical logic or extra biblical authority to convince others their conclusions are correct.

Valid rules of interpretation should accurately reflect the divine architecture which God created. Fortunately for us, we have had 26 centuries of fulfillment that we can use to test our conclusions about fulfilled and unfulfilled events. If the rules are not valid, then there will be no consistency in the interpretation. *Every student of prophecy should test his or her conclusions with something other than a private interpretation or religious bias.* Consider this: If the methods used are not valid, prophetic interpretation becomes like "a nose of wax" which can be manipulated to our satisfaction for political, religious or personal reasons. If this were the case, how could the Bible reveal to us things we do not want to hear? How could the Bible tell us things we do not want to believe?

Any interpretation of prophecy which does not conform to a stated set of valid rules is classified as a "private interpretation." The word "private" does not mean obscure. Millions of people can believe and endorse a private interpretation. A private interpretation is an interpretation which has no external means of validation. In other words, a private interpretation is any interpretation that cannot be tested and validated with a set of stated rules. This brings us back to the need for understanding the apocalyptic architecture in Daniel. There is only one architecture in Daniel and Revelation and there is only one truth and one accurate interpretation of the prophecies. Even if we have the right rules of interpretation, our chances of getting to the intended meaning are not guaranteed, but they are greatly improved! (It is one thing to have the right set of rules, but it is another to correctly apply the rules and reach God's intended meaning.)

Validating a Conclusion

When it comes to solving the unknown, we have no other choice than to rely upon consistent rules that conform with what is known to be true! This is true in every science. For example, the simple equation $2x + 3 = 13$ is solved by using rules of algebra. Since the rules of interpretation for apocalyptic prophecy are not written in the Bible (no rules are declared in nature or any science), the rules must be *derived* and *proven* true with careful research and observation. This statement is critical: *Rules are not invented; rather, man may only discover the presence or operation of rules by repeatedly testing the architecture which God created.* We detect the presence of a rule when we recognize a consistent behavior or architecture. After finding the presence of a rule, it becomes necessary to carefully state the rule so that the behavior can be independently validated by others.

Consider this example: Sir Isaac Newton researched the effects of gravity. He studied the behavior of gravity using different experiments. After observing that gravity behaved in certain consistent ways, he developed an algebraic formula expressing its operation. *Sir Isaac Newton did not make up the rule that governs gravity.* God did that. However, Sir Isaac Newton was able to discover the rule by which gravity operates because the behavior of gravity is constant. Then, Newton expressed the rule of gravity in a manner that allowed others to understand and calculate the effect of gravity. The study of apocalyptic prophecy is very similar to the study of gravity. We have to study and understand "the known" before we can solve "the unknown." Before any conclusions can be trusted, the student has to demonstrate the validity of a set of rules which methodically explain the historical fulfillment of the prophetic elements in Daniel that have already been fulfilled.

Four Rules

Many Christians accept what their leaders say about the fulfillment of prophecy without closely studying the prophecy for themselves. This acceptance is not based on intellectual confirmation. Instead, Christians tend to believe their leaders because they do not know anything else to believe. Of course, the mysteries surrounding Bible prophecy will ultimately vanish during the Great Tribulation because the evidence of what is written in prophecy will be clearly observed. Until the Great Tribulation begins, however, we have to follow the rules. If our rules are valid, the books of Daniel and Revelation will form one unified story. In fact, I have found a comprehensive drama that is in perfect harmony with all of Scripture! The prophetic conclusions presented in this book were produced using the following four rules:

> **1.** Each apocalyptic prophecy has a beginning and ending point in time and the events within each prophecy must occur within the order they are given.

2. A fulfillment of apocalyptic prophecy occurs when all of the specifications within that prophecy are met. This includes the order of events outlined in the prophecy.

3. Apocalyptic language can be literal, symbolic or analogous. To reach the intended meaning of a prophecy, the student must consider: (a) the context, (b) the use of parallel language in the Bible, and (c) relevant statements in the Bible that define that symbol if an element is thought to be symbolic.

4. God reckons apocalyptic time in two ways: (a) a day for a year, and (b) as literal time. The presence or absence of the Jubilee calendar determines how God measures time.

I realize a discussion about rules and methods may not seem important or even necessary, however, the basis for the views presented in this book are more than figments of my imagination. I believe the views presented in this book conform to the four rules above. Do not forget this important point. God sealed up the book of Daniel (hid the keys, the four rules) until *the time of the end* because the message in Daniel and Revelation belongs to the final generation. I believe ours is *the* generation that will experience the Great Tribulation. When it begins, we will be caught up in a horrific contest between good and evil. For this reason, God has unsealed the book of Daniel so that we can understand His plans before He exercises His wrath. When it comes to Bible prophecy, religious affiliation has no bearing. Whether a person is Catholic, Protestant, Jew, Hindu, Moslem or Atheist, everyone who lives during the time of the tribulation will see and experience the truth contained in God's Word. The Bible means what it says, and says what it means. So in the final analysis, prophetic truth is not, nor has it ever been, dependent on the approval or even the understanding of any man (and this includes me).

Larry Wilson

Jesus' Final Victory

For thousands of years, people have wondered why God has allowed the devil to exist. The answer to this question is found in apocalyptic prophecy.  Apocalyptic prophecy traces many battles between Christ and Satan until a final conflict between them erupts. Apocalyptic prophecy predicts that evil will triumph over righteousness for a short time. The good news is that Jesus is coming to overthrow the forces of evil and rescue His children. This 606 page commentary on the apocalyptic prophecies found in Daniel and Revelation will help you understand Satan's last stand and Jesus' final victory.

Bible Stories with End Time Parallels

 *Bible Stories with End Time Parallels* provides encouraging stories of faith from the Bible highlighting end time parallels for the final generation on Earth. This book is an excellent follow-up to *Warning! Revelation is about to be fulfilled.*

Other Books by Larry Wilson. . .

A Study on the Seven Seals and the 144,000
A Study on the Seven Trumpets, Two Witnesses, and Four Beasts

Jesus
The Alpha and The Omega

Jesus, The Alpha and The Omega (280 pages) provides a basic framework to understand Bible prophecy. This framework, based on five essential Bible doctrines, helps the serious student of Bible prophecy appreciate the prophecies of Daniel and Revelation. This compelling book examines Jesus' character, ministry, and example. Cross-references to Bible texts provide a basis for in-depth Bible study.

Daniel
Unlocked for the Final Generation

The book of Daniel was sealed up for the benefit of the final generation. This book explains four "keys" that help unravel the information found in Daniel, as well as Revelation. This book (271 pages) is essential study material for those who are awaited the return of Jesus. Before you can completely understand the book of Revelation, you must understand the foundational concepts developed in the book of Daniel.

Wake Up America Seminars, Inc.
P.O. Box 273
Bellbrook, OH 45305
http://www.wake-up.org
(800) 475-0876

Recorded Seminar Series

Many seminars presented by Larry Wilson have been recorded on DVDs and audio CDs. Audio and video streaming programs are also available at *www.wake-up.org*. Call for a free catalog from the Wake Up America Seminars office at (800) 475-0876 to obtain a listing of current recordings. Many end time subjects are presented in a manner that encourages further Bible study. Recordings include studies on the Bible books of Daniel, Revelation, and Ezekiel.

About the Author

Larry Wilson, Director of Wake Up America Seminars, became a born again Christian after returning from a tour of duty in Vietnam. His understanding of the gospel, the plan of salvation, and the atonement of Jesus Christ has thrilled his soul ever since. He has spent over 40 years intensely studying the prophecies of Daniel and Revelation.

In 1988, he published the first edition of this book and since then, has written several books (over 900,000 books in circulation throughout the world). Along with writing books, Larry Wilson gives seminar presentations, produces video programs which have been broadcast from various locations throughout the United States, and is a guest on radio talk shows.

About the Organization

Wake Up America Seminars (WUAS) is both a non-profit and a non-denominational organization. With God's blessings and the generosity of many people, WUAS has distributed millions of pamphlets, books and tapes around the world since it began in 1988. WUAS is not a church and is not affiliated or sponsored by any religious organization. WUAS does not offer membership of any kind. Its mission is not to convert the world to a point of view. Although WUAS has well defined views on certain biblical matters, its mission is primarily "seed sowing." It promotes the primacy of salvation through faith in Jesus Christ, His imminent return, and is doing its best to encourage people with the good news of the gospel. People of all faiths are invited to study the materials produced by WUAS.

We would like to receive comments about this book
or questions you may have. Please send your comments to us at the address below. Thank you.

Wake Up America Seminars, Inc.
P.O. Box 273
Bellbrook, OH   45305
http://www.wake-up.org
email: *wuas@wake-up.org*